ADVANCED PRAISE FOR *NOT QUITE NIRVANA*

"This is a fresh, lively, warm, interesting and valuable book! You will be happy to add it to your library."
　—Sylvia Boorstein, author of *Happiness Is An Inside Job: Practicing for a Joyful Life*

"*Not Quite Nirvana* will resonate with anyone who has ever tried to juggle more than two things at once. It's an important and joyful book, one that left me comforted, refreshed, and inspired to go out and add more kindness to the world."
　—Tiricn Steinbach, Faculty, Berkeley Initiative for Mindfulness in Law

"Rachel Neumann brings wonderful insights to the practice of meditation and what it means to weave it into our everyday lives. This is a great book, one that can help us find balance as well as a sense of peace and clarity in the midst of it all."
　—Sharon Salzberg, author of *Real Happiness* and *Lovingkindness*

NOT QUITE NIRVANA

NIRVANA

A SKEPTIC'S JOURNEY TO MINDFULNESS

RACHEL NEUMANN
Introduction by Thich Nhat Hanh

PARALLAX
PRESS

Berkeley, California

Parallax Press
P.O. Box 7355
Berkeley, California 94707
www.parallax.org

Parallax Press is the publishing division of the
Unified Buddhist Church, Inc.

Edited by Tai Moses
Cover and text design by Debbie Berne

Neumann, Rachel.
  Not quite nirvana : a skeptic's journey
to mindfulness / by Rachel Neumann ;
introduction by Thich Nhat Hanh.
     pages cm
  ISBN 978-1-937006-23-5
  1. Religious life—Buddhism. 2. Neumann,
Rachel. I. Title.
  BQ5405.N38 2012
  294.3'444—dc23

2012032334

1 2 3 4 5 / 16 15 14 13 12

To Thay, for being available
To Yeshi, who embodies full engagement
And to Osha, the most compassionate of skeptics

Contents

Introduction

THICH NHAT HANH

OVER THE PAST TEN YEARS, Rachel Neumann has edited more than twenty of my books. Thanks to her profound understanding of my teachings, style, and voice, my message has been communicated clearly, correctly, and authentically to thousands of readers. I am deeply grateful for her skillful work and dedication. Over the course of that time, she has learned this critical lesson: Do not get caught in the form of a teaching, but let the heart of your own understanding guide your path. In *Not Quite Nirvana*, Rachel passes on the crucial lesson that your best teacher is your own mindful awareness.

In the Sutra on Knowing the Better Way to Catch a Snake, the Buddha said,

> When a mountain stream overflows and becomes a torrent of floodwater carrying debris, a person who wants to get across might think, "What is the safest way to cross this floodwater?" Assessing the situation, he may decide to gather branches and grasses, construct a raft, and use it to cross to the other side. But, after arriving on the other side, he may think, "I spent a lot of time and energy building this raft. It is a prized

possession, and I will carry it with me as I continue my journey." If he puts it on his shoulders or head and carries it with him on land, do you think that would be intelligent? . . . I have given this teaching on the raft many times to remind you how necessary it is to let go of all the true teachings, not to mention teachings that are not true.

Rachel's journey is full of unabashed appreciation of the joys and sorrows of everyday life. It is also a story of finding a little more peace with aging and death. Many people are afraid of aging; some are even more afraid of aging than of death! But I have found that old age is something very delicious. You are calmer, you go more slowly, and you enjoy much more than when you are very young. You don't rush. You take your time. And you taste every moment of your daily life.

Aging can also give you practice in having the courage to face your eventual death. When you practice acknowledging your fears, you become aware you are still alive, that you still have so many things to treasure and enjoy. Then you will know how to act to make people happy. Wherever you go, you will carry the happiness of a lot of people with you. You will be able to enjoy the sunshine, the fog, the air, the water. Confucius said, "If you don't know how to handle your life, how can you handle your death?" If you can look deeply into death, and see the birthless and deathless nature of you and me and all phenomena, then you will really live a life that is worthwhile.

In this moment, there are many cells dying in me and in you. We don't have time to organize funerals for them; there are so many of them dying. Many new cells are also being born; we don't have enough time to celebrate their birth. Death cannot be without birth. The death of something is also the birth of something. *Not Quite Nirvana* offers insights in how to live fully each day with this knowledge. Amidst all the busyness and chaos, it is possible to celebrate the myriad possibilities of the present moment.

Thich Nhat Hanh
June 2012

PART I

Available

1. A Skeptic's Guide to Mindfulness

I AM ON A SAGE-COVERED MOUNTAINTOP deep in the Southern California desert, walking past a small, green lotus pond. All around me, people are dressed in grays and browns, walking slowly, and speaking in whispers. Every few moments the ringing of a huge bronze bell fills the air and everyone stands still and silent, slight smiles on many of their faces, frozen in a tableau of serenity until the bell fades. I fill my lungs with the warm mountain air, trying to release the claustrophobic tightness in my chest. I look longingly at the dirt road that leads away from the monastery, desperate for a crowded bar, an old pool table, and an early-nineties hip-hop soundtrack. But the bell rings again. Now it is time for a silent lunch. Restraining myself from running or skipping, I walk as slowly as I can toward the dining hall.

Just two years earlier, in the fall of 2002, I was living in a fourth-floor Brooklyn walkup, extremely pregnant, and looking for a way to return to the San Francisco Bay Area. I was brought up on a rural California commune, surrounded by trees, mountains, rivers, and a roving gang of other dirty, half-naked children. Jason, my partner, grew up on a small family farm where he took care of goats, cows, and sheep. He fed them, groomed them, and, when it was necessary, helped them give birth. One of the best things about our dissimilar childhoods was the connection we both had to the earth and to close-knit community. We wanted our kids to have at least a little of those things.

At the same time, Zen Master Thich Nhat Hanh was looking for a Bay Area–based editor for his publishing house. I'd interviewed Thich Nhat Hanh in New York a year earlier, just weeks after the World Trade Center attacks, and the interview had stuck with me. When I heard he was looking for an editor, I promptly went out and bought every one of his books I could find. I stayed inside for a week and read them all. Then I applied for the job. Within a few months, I was working full-time as his personal editor as well as editing the work of a number of other Buddhist teachers. I brought my baby to work with me in a sling and learned as I went along about Buddhism, mindfulness, colic, and how to function on two hours of sleep.

Clearly, I had a lot to learn. What, for example, was an "equality complex," and how could that possibly be bad? How could one live in the present moment and still get anything done? What was with Buddhism's fixation on numbers? There was the one vehicle, two dimensions, three jewels, four noble truths, five mindfulness trainings, six paramitas, seven virtues, and the eightfold path. My head was spinning. I'd thought Buddhism was about making things simple! Somehow, through it all, I was supposed to be paying attention to my breath. Unfortunately, every time I took a deep breath, I thought I might pass out from exhaustion.

I could have easily won a Buddhist trivia contest (Name the Buddha's first five disciples! How many hell realms are there? First prize winner gets a bowl full of emptiness!), but I didn't feel like I was learning anything that would help me get through the day. What I needed was a mindfulness practice, a way to translate what I was learning into body knowledge.

His students and friends called Thich Nhat Hanh, "Thay," which means "teacher" in Vietnamese, but I couldn't say it without feeling like an imposter. I'd been raised a firm atheist and I'd seen friends get swept into cults that damaged them and their families for years. As an adult, calling anyone "teacher" without question seemed a bad idea. I have a built-in wariness of anyone who offers a particular path to happiness. Instead, I've found inspiration in the way individuals and groups stay true to their own intentions and principals instead of relying on an outside arbiter, even when it's hard.

Thich Nhat Hanh has said that all Buddhism is academic without practice. Despite my skepticism, the daily demands of work and family life, and my continued strong aversion to sitting still, I have slowly found ways to practice what I was preaching. My understanding of mindfulness is forged both from Buddhist practice and from the daily intensity of parenting. Luna and Plum, my two daughters, have humbled and honed every truth I think I know. Whatever I've learned intellectually has been held to the daily test of their questions, challenges, and needs. The mess of parenthood, getting older, and the challenges of daily life haven't been impediments to mindful awareness; they are the foundation of it. Every mindfulness teaching should come with a big warning on it: *Try this at home.*

Mindfulness is a deep awareness of both the singularity and transience of the present moment. It's an extremely useful tool. This past year, my youngest daughter started school, my father and my partner were quite ill, Thay turned eighty-six, and I turned forty. Practicing mindfulness did not make these transitions easy or without sadness and fear. But it has increased my daily awareness of my own happiness, helped me build and keep a strong and caring community around me, and helped me come to a more graceful truce with two of my greatest fears: aging and death.

When change and loss come at me in wave after wave, I found three questions that help me keep my breath. The first is *Am I available?* Is my mind somewhere else or do I have attention for what is right in front of me? The second question is *Am I engaged?* Am I aware of how I influence this moment or just waiting for it to pass? The third question is *Am I connected?* What is my relationship to other living beings around me and the causes and conditions that created this moment? These questions tether me to what is happening in the present moment.

I see Thich Nhat Hanh no more than once or twice a year. Usually, our meeting is squeezed in between his traveling, teaching, and caring for over 250 monks and nuns around the world. When he is not travelling, he is writing books, leading retreats, gardening, and spending a good part of each day engaged in sitting and walking meditation. Still, each time we are together the moment contains the same stillness and focus as when we first met.

The rest of the time, I work with words and try them at home. I send manuscripts to Plum Village, the meditation center in France where he makes his home, and his attendant emails me back his comments. I sit with what I'm learning. Chewing over the words, sometimes I swallow them and sometimes I spit them out. Thich Nhat Hanh and I aren't an obvious pairing, but it works. He is not my only teacher or inspiration, but now, without irony and with a smaller measure of self-consciousness, I call him Thay.

I'm not at peace with everything. The sufferings of aging, death, and injustice still feel like suffering, and sometimes the pleasures still pass too quickly. But there is a spaciousness in each day, and more time that is filled with an easy and relaxed joy. Returning again and again to mindful awareness has taught me to come home to myself in this world that often seems far from nirvana. I've discovered that each of us is more deeply connected to each other than we may have noticed, and we are capable of powerful joy and transformation, both separately and together.

2. Fake It Till You Make It

WHEN I MET THICH NHAT HANH, it was two weeks after the September 11 attacks and New York felt raw. The air had turned cold. Posters of the missing were stapled to every telephone pole, though they were starting to be covered over with flyers for concert promotions. People were both friendlier and more anxious than they had been before the attacks. They offered their seats to strangers on the train and jumped at the sound of car alarms.

My editor at the *Village Voice* had asked me to compile the response from various authors and public figures to the attacks. Did these people recommend an immediate military response or was there another way? I interviewed writers, politicians, and spiritual leaders. Since the Vietnamese Buddhist monk Thich Nhat Hanh had just written a book on anger and was speaking at Riverside Church, I went to interview him.

It was hot for late September and I was sweaty, wishing I'd had time to change. I was distracted by the crowd and my thoughts of the dinner I needed to rush to right after the interview. The venerable gothic cathedral was full of people in street clothes and others in brown monastic robes. The two groups glided past each other, one busy and chattering, the other busy and silent. The Vietnamese and Western monastics, with their shaved heads and monochromatic robes, looked more fashionable than the New Yorkers.

I went up to the first person willing to catch my eye—a tall, thin monk whose scalp shone in the bright overhead lights. I explained why I was there, and he nodded and motioned for me to follow him. Two nuns came out of the crowd to accompany us. We walked, a nun in front of me and a nun behind, upstairs to an unmarked door. The monk knocked gently. Another nun answered the door and gestured for me to be seated. The room smelled like incense and candles.

Across from me, in front of a thick stack of calligraphy paper and a jar of black ink, sat Thich Nhat Hanh. Sitting was all he was doing. He wasn't vacant or unaware, stoned or spaced out. He wasn't striking an enlightened pose. He didn't seem preoccupied or full of particularly deep thoughts, and he didn't seem as if he were waiting for me, although he wasn't doing anything else. He was just, profoundly, *there*.

Having known Thich Nhat Hanh for ten years now, his solid presence continues to be what impresses me most. It is a quiet thing and more startling for its quietness. Whether we are in the middle of a meeting to plan a book, eating lunch, or having a picnic at the beach, his sense of thereness remains; he is present in this moment, listening, without preconceptions about what will happen in the next moment or how things should go.

I'd mostly experienced the feeling of being fully present after moments of intense joy or sorrow, when strong emotions have swept through and flooded whatever thoughts, worries, and preoccupations normally inhabit me. Afterward, everything would look brighter and more clear.

Meeting Thay was a realization that it might be possible to reach clarity without first needing catharsis. In fact, after meeting Thay that first time, I tried to reproduce that state of serenity and clarity in my daily interactions with other people. In the subway, at the deli counter, whenever people were yelling at me to move along or to hurry up and pay, I presented my most placid face and beatific smile, and silently and serenely went about my businesses. Usually, people backed off, but probably just because they thought I was creepy.

No wonder it didn't work. I had no practice of meditation or mindfulness behind my look. I should have known. Whenever I deliberately try for a look, I fail. As I smiled serenely on the disgruntled New Yorkers, I was reminded of a time in college when I was determined to seduce a young man who I really liked with a wise and sultry look. I didn't have much experience being wise and sultry, but I had some ideas from watching movies and was sure I could pull it off.

After practicing in the mirror for a couple of weeks, I felt confident enough to try it one day in the cafeteria. My crush was in the drinks line. I walked up behind him and nonchalantly grabbed a plastic cup. As I filled it with ice, I tilted my head, sucked in my cheeks, stuck out my lower lip, widened my eyes and, through gritted teeth, gave him a husky, "Hello."

He looked genuinely concerned. "Are you okay?" he asked. "You look sick."

"I'm fine," I said in my most breathy voice, "just a little dizzy." I was, in fact getting dizzy. My sucked-in cheeks and protruding lower lip were making it difficult to get enough air into my lungs. My crush stepped back, trying to fill his cup with orange juice while staying as far away from me as possible. "Get better soon!" he said, scurrying away.

Later, a friend tried to console me. "Don't try so hard," she said. "You're much more charming when you're not trying to be." It was true then and it's true now. I'm also much more present when I'm not working so hard at it. If I'm trying hard for serenity, then I've already failed. As Thich Nhat Hanh reminds me, being mindful shouldn't take a lot of grunting effort. Practice and attention are critical, yes, but the feeling should be of ease, not strain. Strive for relaxed diligence," Thay has said, "rather than effort." Diligence implies committed practice; effort implies difficult work. I am reminded of the many New York yoga classes I attended, where everyone sweats and grits their teeth in an effort to relax the hardest.

Despite Thay's steady reminders to the contrary, I was still sure serenity was something for which I could learn a secret formula, the same way I'd finally figured out social graces. On the commune there hadn't been much focus on manners. When I started attending a city elementary school, I was most drawn to the other kids who, often because they didn't have many adults at home, knew how to take care of themselves. Like me, they walked home by themselves and made their own lunches. But they also knew things I didn't, such as how to talk to the clerk at the drugstore so she'd offer us a free sample of the hard candy. They taught me important things my parents hadn't, such as that saying "please" and "thank you" made grown-ups like you and leave you alone. They taught me what politeness and coolness looked like. After meeting Thay, I felt like I knew for the first time what peacefulness looked like. I figured it couldn't be that different. If I just asked around, surely I could learn the tools and secret tips I needed to get there.

3. A Revolting Monk

WHEN I FIRST ARRIVED at my new job as an editor of Buddhist books, seven months pregnant and eager to learn everything I could from a true Zen master, I was disappointed to find he wasn't there. I lumbered up to my light-filled attic office and found an empty swivel chair, bare walls, a buzzing fly, and a desk covered under a barricade of dusty cardboard boxes overflowing with paper. Each piece of paper was covered in the forceful black indentations of an old typewriter. Not only was there no monk around to teach me the meaning of the Lotus Sutra, there was no previous editor around to show me how one could possibly edit a book on it.

On top of one of the precariously perched boxes was a note from the publisher telling me he'd gone to Germany and would be back in a couple of weeks. Thich Nhat Hanh was in Plum Village. He could be reached via email, through his attendant, and we'd meet up when he next came to the United States, in six months or so.

There was an assistant editor sitting in the next room, who welcomed me with a nice smile. She also warned me that the temporary freelance editor they'd been using, who had a doctorate in Eastern Religion, had inserted terminology from the

Theravada tradition into the last manuscript. "Just something to watch out for," she warned, "when doing a book of commentaries on a Mahayana sutra."

I did what I always do when I'm out of my depth: I read. I read in bed, at work, and at stoplights. Some of the chapters read like talks at a party I wasn't invited to, and I skimmed them lightly, brushing past paragraphs on other dimensions, previous Buddha incarnations, and the whole idea that "form is emptiness and emptiness is form." Others seemed to say the same thing over and over again: Inhale. Exhale. Enjoy the present moment. Repeat.

After reading through pages and pages of manuscripts and published books, listening to recordings of talks, and asking many questions of my patient coworkers, Thich Nhat Hanh's voice was lodged firmly in my head whether I wanted it there or not. I was ready to begin. The first two of his books I was supposed to work on were about building community. I read each page reverently and kept my editing as light as possible. I was like a housecleaner in a fancy home, tidying up here and there, perhaps washing out a particularly muddled paragraph or trimming the edges of a sentence, but certainly not rearranging the furniture. Would Thay notice how I caught those mistakes or fixed those sentences? Would he be pleased?

I left work after two months to give birth to my daughter Luna and came back four weeks later, with Luna wrapped across my chest in a sling or sleeping in the baby hammock I'd brought to the office. One day, as I was nursing and editing a chapter on our interconnectedness with all of life, I came across this line; "When I was younger," Thich Nhat Hanh said, "I was a revolting monk." A revolting monk? Somehow I doubted it.

That one line was enough to remind me that the words weren't as precious as the meaning behind them. Most of what I had to work with were talks that had been transcribed and sometimes translated from French or Vietnamese, or from Vietnamese to French and then to English. To make it not only comprehensible, but also inviting, I had to be willing to dig under the words, move them around, and not mistake the words for the teaching that lay within them.

If I could just figure out what Thay meant, then I could figure out how to make it make sense to someone who was hearing it for the first time. I read the paragraph again and again. It was a story of youthful impatience and how to turn judgment into action. This was something I wanted to understand. This was something I needed to learn. As I changed "revolting" to "rebellious," I realized that the key to editing was going to be listening deeply, listening behind the words, and that my beginner's mind, if I was willing to be patient and diligent with it, was a fine place to start.

4. Are You Available?

WHILE THAY WAS gently encouraging me to pay attention at work, my children were demanding I pay attention when I got home. My mother is a midwife and I had been at many home and hospital births before having Luna and Plum. I had helped care for a roving band of smaller children on the commune and been the caretaker of my eight-years-younger sister for much of her young life while both my parents worked. I was thirty-two, not particularly young, and I had longed to be pregnant for at least a year before it happened. Despite all this, I was shocked by the reality of parenthood. Some tiny, squalling being had suddenly been put bull's-eye in the center of my universe.

This Copernican shift meant that I was often forced to pay attention. No matter how tired or hungry or uncomfortable I was, this small person's own tiredness, hunger, or discomfort required my full attention. Despite her size, she created a cacophony for the senses. I was surrounded by the smells of sweet and sour milk, the warmth of a soft body, the eerie beauty of her tiny face, and the loud cries of the present moment.

Before I had kids, I was determined that, when I did have them, I would not get completely absorbed in them. I would love them and be attached to them, but that wouldn't preclude the other work I was doing or lessen the truth that everyone was somebody's precious child and deserving of getting their physical and emotional needs met. Whenever I'd thought of having a child, I'd imagined a ten-year-old. I hadn't counted on how a child's infanthood could be such a singularly engulfing and need-intensive time. Lack of sleep and the steep learning curve of parenting meant that I often felt as if other things in the world were happening very far away. I'd fasten my seat belt and drive to work, eating leftover baby cereal or reading through a manuscript at the red lights, but I did these things as if underwater.

Perhaps if I'd had those kinds of babies that sleep well and often, who mew instead of wail, and who spend those first three months smiling blissfully in their sleep as if they are still in their "fourth trimester" outside of the womb, I would have experienced this time differently. But both my kids were the kind of babies who came into the world with their eyes wide open and were loathe to close them. Before Luna, I'd imagined being the kind of parent who threw her baby into a sling and brought her to every party, meeting, and protest. Instead, Luna needed lots of quiet or she broke into wailing. Even trips in the car or the sound of the vacuum cleaner, which babies are supposed to love, sent her into long fits of tears. The only surefire way to calm her was to curl her up in a sling and keep moving. Plum also came into the world shouting. Although she cried less, she was sick more often, requiring again that the parties, meetings, and protests had to wait.

Then, they started preschool and their teacher taught them an invaluable tool for getting help. They were shown how to put a hand on my shoulder (or hip, or wherever they could reach) and ask me if I was available. The first time Luna did this, I was at the sink. I had come home from work and my work shirt was stained with some unidentifiable child goo that I was trying to wash off. Luna reached up and touched my back and I turned around to ask her, with a sigh, what she needed. But before I could, she asked me, "Mama, are you available?"

I was startled. Was I available? I actually wasn't but I hadn't realized until then that it was a perfectly fine option to say so. I was doing something already. "No," I told her. "I'm not. But I will be when I'm finished washing this shirt."

Asking this question served two lovely purposes. First, the asking reminded me that I always have a choice about where to put my awareness. Basically, my kids were asking if I was present enough to help them out. When they asked, I had to ask myself. This meant that I was immediately more in the moment than I'd been before they asked. Second, because the question gave me a moment to think, they usually got a calmer and more honest answer, even if not always a positive one.

Before we discovered the "available" question, I often felt trapped and irritable when my kids asked for or demanded help. I would either help them and be cranky about it because I really was right in the middle of doing something else, or not help them but repeatedly say "just a second" as they asked over and over again, until one of us had a meltdown.

Jason and I, after twenty years together, have also found we get better results if we ask each other if we're available before we jump in. This doesn't mean constantly checking in. But if I'm saying something that's hard I want to make sure he's listening before rambling on. It doesn't work to ask, "Are you available to take out the trash?" That's cheating, because what I really mean is not "Are you available?" but "I want you to take out the trash." The real question is, are you awake? Are you too focused on something else to take in what I'm saying right now? If that's the case, then we try to wait until the person is actually available before getting to the specifics.

Most people in the world will not ask you if you're available before they interrupt you with their own needs and desires or tell you what they think you should be doing. The question, "Are you available?" works like a stop sign. It is a reminder to pause and check in.

The trick, the hard part, is to stop for a moment before responding even if the other person doesn't ask or notice if I'm available and runs the stop sign. Jason, an artist and a carpenter, sees this question as the break in the machine between stimulus and response. We've evolved, for ease and safety's sake, to react without thinking. This is great for life-threatening situations, so I can throw my body in front of the wild bear trying to attack my little child or jump out of the way of the careening car. But it works less well in everyday situations, when my child throws a rock at a car, when a coworker snaps, when an unexpected bill comes in the mail, when I'm getting bumped into or pushed past, or when my attention wanders in myriad tiny ways each day.

Unless I first ask myself if I'm available, I often deal reluctantly with the situation in front of me. Or I don't deal with it, and un-consciously ignore it or deny it's happening. I pretend not to see the person on the street. Or I respond sharply to the person at work and then make up for it by doing something I really didn't want to do. If I don't decide on my own availability, I feel put upon and rushed, without ever having simply decided what I am doing. It's true that, even if I'm available, I have to deal with things I don't enjoy. But at least, if I've made a conscious choice to deal with something, I handle it with a little more grace.

Sometimes it works to put my hand at the top of my scapula, where my shoulder meets my neck, to remind me to take a con-scious breath. The length of that one inhale and exhale is often all the pause I have in which to decide if I'm available, before I have to deal with the situation. It can be enough. Touching that same spot on the top of my shoulder now triggers a mindful stop. The more I practice, the more that reflection becomes habit, and the less likely I am to lash out. There is always some element of choice in what I'm doing and if I consciously make that choice, I spend less energy thinking of what's wrong with the other person for interrupting me and more energy enjoying the moment in front of me.

The story goes that when Siddhartha, the man who became known as the Buddha, went out into the world from his pro-tected palace, he saw all kinds of suffering. The more he traveled, the more he also saw all kinds of potential for joy. Wherever he went, though, he saw people sleepwalking, going through the motions of their lives without fully experiencing them. The

Buddha wasn't a god or the instrument of a god. He was a human being who, as the story goes, woke up. "Buddha" means "the Awakened One" in Sanskrit. When someone asks me if I'm available, or when I ask myself this same question, I am being nudged to wake up to what is happening in me and around me and to fully experience it before it is gone.

5. Deep Listening

WHEN I WAS FOUR, my family moved from an isolated river valley to the city. We bounced around between different communal houses before landing in a duplex in North Oakland. Our house was near the Oakland and Berkeley border and sat between two very different worlds. One block to the West was Telegraph Avenue, with a liquor store on our corner, a bar across the street, and a Jack-in-the-Box with a huge menacing clown on its sign that I could see from my bedroom window. It was on Telegraph that I bought candy bars at the liquor store and stepped around the drunk guys sleeping on the bench while waiting for the bus to school. Ten blocks to the East was the Elmwood neighborhood of Berkeley, where I would buy a small perfectly-potted succulent for my father each year on his birthday, stare through windows at oriental rugs and turquoise jewelry, and spend hours in the boutiques using the testers of the sweet-smelling body lotions and potions until they kicked me out.

Because both these worlds were new to me, I spent a lot of time listening to the different ways people spoke and what they spoke about. When people at school would argue over whose neighborhood was tougher, I knew enough to side with the people arguing for North Oakland vs. East Oakland, though we rarely went to East Oakland. I could also make myself close to invisible in Elmwood, sneaking into the small stores and sometimes leaving with a little something—a barrette or a marble.

I became adept at listening to several conversations at once while also doing something else because it was a good way of surviving the new worlds I now lived in. That conversational restlessness stayed with me until working as an editor for various Buddhist authors started to slow me down almost against my will. Unless I listened deeply to their words and their different voices, I couldn't edit. I had to read everything a few times, and much more slowly than my usual method of devouring a book while doing three other things at the same time. Often I had questions and there was no one to give me an immediate answer, so I'd go back and read the paragraph again until it made sense.

This was particularly challenging when I was working with ideas I didn't agree with. At the time I started editing Thay's writing, I had just started eating meat again after many years as a vegetarian. On the commune, the only food option was what was put in front of us. When there was meat it was usually because one of our animals had been killed. As I was pretty attached to our animals, I soon become a vegetarian, eating mostly rice, yogurt, and molasses. When we moved to the city, I tried bacon and salami for the first time, and made them the exception to my vegetarian diet for the rest of my childhood, before becoming fully vegetarian again after I left home. Then, while pregnant, I started eating meat regularly, making sure it came from the most healthy and ethical sources I could find. At the same time, Thay had just gone from being a vegetarian to being vegan and eating no animal products at all. He would write about the importance of not eating animal products for the health of the planet, and I would help make sure the words formed a persuasive paragraph while at the same time I was happily munching on my hardboiled eggs and salami sandwich, and feeling lucky to have it. Thay would write about the importance of drinking no alcohol whatsoever and I would sit there in the evening with my glass of wine and a pen, crossing out some lines and moving others around.

I wanted to soften his words. I was so tempted to insert some exceptions. What about people who didn't have access to fresh produce? What about the difference between pasture-raised animals and small family farms compared to big factory farms? Could one very occasional glass of wine really hurt? I wanted to open up what he was saying so that people like me, and others even less focused on health concerns, wouldn't feel excluded or judged and miss the other parts.

But my job as his editor was to listen and make clear what he was saying, not to say what I wanted to say. I had to read the words again and again to hear what was behind what he was saying. How could this be said so that it came out as concern, instead of judgment? I could judge the effectiveness of my edits by whether or not I had made the author's argument strong enough that I started to agree with it, or at least understand it.

Then my children became devout vegetarians. We were leaving a Thai restaurant when Plum turned to me and said, "Mama, is chicken satay made from dead chickens?"

I told her it was. Since Plum cries over the death of a blood-sucking mosquito and mourns for the lice I've found in her hair, I had an idea where this was going.

"Is all meat made from dead animals?" she wanted to know. Yes, I told her, all meat.

"Then I'm not eating it again," she said. "I don't want to eat dead animals." It was that clear for her. Sometimes, after all the arguments with Thay in my head, something can become that clear, that quickly. Luna immediately joined her, and the two of them have been steadfast in their decision not to eat meat for years now, despite the temptations.

Often when I ask Plum to take a deep breath when she is upset, she responds, "I can breathe while I talk!" I used to have that same attitude about listening. I'd kept the childhood habit of always having one ear in the conversations around me, even as I carried on my own conversation. I could listen while I thought about my grocery list or the bump on my forehead. I could even listen while I read my email, ate an apple, and tied my child's shoe at the same time. I thought this was working for me, for the most part, but at some point I noticed that, by not fully listening, I was missing out on something besides the actual words the other person was saying.

It's hard enough to read without judging or being tempted to insert my own opinions when I'm working with a book manuscript. But listening in order to deeply understand other live human beings, whose words are always mixed with their own questions, emotions, and judgments, is a lot harder. Listening to other living, breathing human beings can be inconvenient and time-consuming. I tend to talk and think fast. So sometimes when other people talk, if I'm not paying attention, I jump ahead to the end of their sentence in my mind. Then, I'm so busy trying not to interrupt with the answer to what they're clearly working their way to asking, that I forget they're talking and I start doing something else.

Thich Nhat Hanh and I recently spent a year working on a book called *Fidelity* that focused on some of the tools for successful long-term relationships. We had some difference of opinion at times, as his sixty-plus years as a celibate monk and my twenty-five-plus years in romantic relationships gave us rather different perspectives on the importance of passion. For the most part, we worked it out. *Fidelity* is worth reading in its entirety, but here, in a couple of lines, is what I learned from it. If you want to make your relationship work, you are going to have to give up listening as an activity that can be multi-tasked. It's really inconvenient not to be able to listen while making a grocery list or cleaning or eating, but the listening goes a whole lot better if you listen when you're available.

Jason's mother's people were stoic working farmers who immigrated from Northern Europe. They worked hard on the land and spoke little. I'm from formerly poor and then middle class Eastern European and German Jews many of whom became professors. They valued critical thinking and language above almost all. So it's not surprising we have very different approaches to talking and listening, along with some stereotypical gender differences. I am often in the position of wanting Jason to talk more, to say more, to tell me what he is feeling. He is often in the position of wanting me to talk less, say less, and leave him alone to feel whatever he is feeling. It used to be that the more I wanted him to talk, the more I'd talk in an effort to bombard him into talking, and the less I'd listen. I thought he had to talk first, and *then* I'd listen. But watching Thay, I realized the opposite was true. He listened first, and that gave people the space to talk when they were ready.

Thay says, "The practice of deep listening can help people say the things they have never been able to say. The most precious opportunity is to be heard by someone who has the capacity to listen." For me and Jason, this has meant less time pretending to listen and a little more time actually listening. It turned out that although I've always thought I was pretty good at pretend listening, he could tell. He knew I was just impatiently waiting for him to finish so I could get my advice in. The lawyer in me is hard to silence, but my intention isn't to win the argument or to be right; it's to connect. Thay says, "Even if we hear something that is not true, we continue to listen deeply so the other person can express his pain. If we reply to correct him, the practice will not bear fruit."* It turns out that listening is lot like beginning a meditation practice: It's painful, especially in the beginning, and

* Thich Nhat Hanh, *Answers from the Heart* (Berkeley, CA: Parallax Press, 2011).

shouldn't be done for long periods of time. But it can also be very refreshing and effortless, like sitting in warm sunlight.

Sometimes I can't listen or I just don't want to. I'm tired or distracted or the day has just been too much. Then I am learning to say that I'm not available, instead of pretending. Jason is better at this than I am. He will say, "I just want to sleep" or "I really don't have the energy right now." I'll get mad at him, but less mad than when he pretends to listen and nods or agrees without having any real idea what I'm saying. I rarely say I can't listen; I'm too curious and don't want to miss anything. I want to find answers and make things better. If I just listen, I worry that listening won't be "enough" and that things will never change. But I'm learning it's better if I wait. I'm slowly building a trust in the process of deep listening. It may or may not be enough, depending on the situation, but it is almost always the first step toward understanding.

I believe strongly in decisive action and quick thinking. It takes vigilant awareness to listen deeply and still function with the level of quick reflexes and intensity my daily life requires. I think Thay would say I need to slow down. But I don't have any desire for more slowness. I want to be able to move at my own pace. To do that, I need to listen to my own instincts. Rather than not judging, I want my kids to learn to listen to themselves that they can trust their judgment. This is important for their own safety. They need to be able to think quickly and make quick decisions to know when and how to avoid someone that possibly means them harm, when to cross the street, and when to yell for help. Listening deeply to themselves will help them figure out who is a friend they can count on, who they will love, and what work they should do.

Recently, all the parents of second graders at Luna's school were called in for a meeting about our children. We sat there listening as the psychologists introduced themselves and talked about the social and emotional development of eight-year-olds and their growing tendency to create hierarchies. Finally, a parent anxiously burst out with what many of us were thinking, "But why are we here? What did we do?" Before we could listen to anything, we needed to know: Are we in trouble? Did we do something wrong? We couldn't listen while we were anxious and concerned about our own welfare.

One of the most important things I've learned from listening to Thay and listening to my children is how critically important it is that I listen to myself. The more I listen, the more likely I am to go for a run or lock myself in my room, rather than explode or collapse. And the more adept I get at listening to myself, the more space and attention I have for listening to other people. With friends, I now find it easier to step back and listen. With Jason, it's also getting easier. But when it comes to my children, as they've gotten older, I find deep listening to be more difficult than when they were babies. Perhaps this is because I've known them since I could listen to them without words, and now they're full of words that often distract me from what they're feeling. Partly this is because I also have my own childhood experiences that color how I see theirs. Listening to them is a lot harder than keeping them safe, teaching them, and showering them with affection. I believe my job as a parent is in large part to teach them to take care of themselves, and yet my instinctive response to when I listen deeply to their suffering is to want to jump in and fix it. While I know that expressing their disappointment, embarrassment, suffering, and pain is necessary for their strength and their joy, it's still hard sometimes to listen to it.

∾

One spring morning after a light rain, when Luna was eight, she found a slug on our front steps and wanted to throw it into the city compost bucket. Usually, she gets ten cents for every slug she throws in, and five cents for every snail. But this morning, we were late to school, and we didn't have time for the slug ritual. I told her we had to leave that slug for now and it would either be there when she got back from school or (hopefully) eaten by a blackbird. This made Plum, who was four at the time, start to cry because she didn't want the slug to have to die.

Luna was fine with the slug's death, but not willing to lose her dime. She began with the most common refrain of all school-age children: "It's not fair," she said. She needed that ten cents and was going to buy something wonderful with it. She continued to chant, "It'snotfairit'snotfairit'snotfairit'snotfair" over and over again, until it became one long high-pitched whine for the first full ten minutes of the car ride. For two minutes, I was irritated. She was being unreasonable. It was just a slug and there would be plenty more. But then I got into her chant, took each sentence as an opportunity to listen and to breathe. After a few more minutes, though, I was done. There was no more enjoying it and I was starting to get itchy. Ten minutes can be a very long time. I told her I was sorry I rushed her and that she could keep going, but I was no longer available and now was going to listen to the radio. She nodded, and then continued for another five minutes, though in a softer tone, enjoying the sound of her own complaint. I had done all I could do and, knowing that, was also able to enjoy the rest of the ride.

As a parent, every suffering that my children experience hits me hard. They have been, compared to many children in the world, incredibly unimaginably lucky. They have seen but not been touched by physical violence. They have never been truly hungry. And although they know people who have been home-less, they themselves have never slept out on the street. Yet the awareness of sufferings, both the inevitable personal ones and the very unnecessary global ones, creep in. They make a sign that says "Sharing Is Caring" and carry it to a protest about unfair lending practices at a bank. They hold bake sales to raise money for earthquake victims. They write letters to governments asking them to protect forests for orangutans. Plum asks, "Did we save the orangutans yet?" There are so many heartbreaking truths about unfairness and violence they have yet to learn.

I sometimes get upset when my children are upset, but it's not just because I love them and want them to be happy. If that was all, I'd be sad when they were sad, but I wouldn't get so angry or frustrated. I get upset in part because I know there are so many sufferings they have yet to experience that I can't fix. When Plum tells me that she is terrified of dying or when Luna says she is lonely on the schoolyard, I think of what tools I can help them learn now, so that they will both be able to make peace with their own sufferings and feel empowered to try and change the larger world ones.

Listening deeply is still one of the most important things I can do and teach them to do. The more space I give to listening to my kids, the clearer my understanding is of what I need to do next. And if they can learn to listen to themselves, to know if something feels right or safe or fair, and if they can learn to truly listen to others, then they too will have a clearer path to action.

I can't stop Plum's fear of dying, but I can make sure we have time to learn how the body works. I can't stop Luna's loneliness, but I can listen to what it feels like. The fear and loneliness will come, so it's good to get to know them. I can share with Luna that sitting on the yard by yourself, breathing deeply and looking at a tree, can sometimes turn the loneliness into the good kind of solitude. I can share with Plum that as soon as I acknowledge that I'm scared, sometimes that helps me be a little less scared.

The Buddha encouraged all of his students to cultivate the three energies of mindfulness (*smrti* in Sanskrit), concentration (*samadhi*), and insight (*prajna*). I'd always thought the words looked beautiful together, and sounded good, but with deep listening, they were starting to make sense. Mindfulness (more open awareness and availability to the present moment) leads to concentration (deep listening, focus), and this can lead to insight (the clarity and understanding of what to do next).

There were many advantages to all the freedom I had as a child, and to my parents more *laissez-faire* parenting style. I got to play in an old dump truck, eat dirt, make my own yogurt, and fall asleep late while the grown-ups danced to Marvin Gaye and Bob Marley. But there wasn't a lot of time together spent on stopping and listening. When I was upset, they were quick to reassure me that everything would "all work out" and then focus on whatever exciting thing was happening next. Once we'd moved to the city, I often felt ill-equipped to deal with the half-drunk men who waited at the bus stop on my way to school, or the kids at school who made fun of my bright colored and heavily-patched clothes or the earnest way I talked. My parents would nod and make sympathetic sounds, and all I wanted was for them to jump on a horse and go punch the kid who was teasing me, or at least teach me how to make a tight fist. I didn't just want someone to be sorry, I wanted to be safe at school and in my own home. If that wasn't possible, I at least wanted the listening to be a solace that helped bolster me for when I had to go back out into the hard places.

In Buddhist iconography, there is a *bodhisattva,* a being of great compassion who lives to relieve the suffering of others, named Avalokiteshvara. This bodhisattva has one thousand arms and hands. There is an eye in the palm of each hand. In the stories about Avalokiteshvara, the eye in the palm represents understanding and the hand represents action. Thay says, "The practice of

Avalokiteshvara is to listen very deeply to every kind of sound, including the sounds of pain from within and from without."[*] Likewise: "When you understand a situation or a person, any action you do will help and you will not cause more suffering. When you have an eye in your hand, you will know how to practice true nonviolence."[**] Listening, understanding, and action go hand in hand.

I still tend to overreact and err on the side of action over understanding. As soon as I stop and listen to my loved one's pain, I want to jump on my horse and grab my sword to slay whoever has done them wrong. I have to remind myself to sit still and breathe and let them finish their story. Sometimes, when I listen with compassion this way, I can get insight into how to help. Other times, if I really listen and wait long enough, I find that often my kids don't need my help. They figure out their own answers, using the tricks I've passed on, modifying them, and finding their own I would never have thought of. They are learning, much sooner than I did, that if they take the time to listen deeply to themselves, insight will come. Their joy, when they figure it out themselves, is enough usually to keep me from rushing in. I'm learning to listen first. When the listening is enough, it's enough. When it's not, and they need more tools, I'm happy to give them a leg up on the horse, lend them my sword, and push them in the right direction to fight their own battles. Of course, I'll ride back up, just in case they need someone to listen to them as they ride.

[*] Thich Nhat Hanh, *Teachings on Love* (Berkeley, CA: Parallax Press, 2007).
[**] ———, *For a Future to Be Possible* (Berkeley, CA: Parallax Press, 2007).

6. Sitting and Stopping

THICH NHAT HANH makes it sound as if awareness is as easy and effortless as soaking beans in water. "You don't need to push the water to enter the bean," he has told me. "You let the bean be in the water, and slowly, slowly the water is absorbed. Overnight the bean gets soaked, swollen, and tender. You are like these mung beans and awareness is the water. The practice is to bring your mind gently back to the present moment with your body and unify body and mind. The tension will slowly dissipate, your awareness will grow, and you can see things in a clearer way."

It's a lot harder to feel like a bean soaking in water when I'm moving. Although I hate to slow down, even for a moment, I've found it helps to stop. I don't mean stopping in some deep metaphorical sense. I mean just physically stopping. If I'm out on the street, this means I stop moving my legs and stand still for a moment, or find a place to sit down. If I'm talking, this means to stop talking. If I'm at work, this means putting my hands in my lap for a few moments and not looking busy. If I'm home, cleaning, organizing, or cooking, this means sitting down without a book or a magazine or a drawing in front of me.

I remember as a child going with my mother to visit a friend of hers at a big white house in Berkeley. We knocked on the heavy wood door and there was no answer. The friend was expecting us, and so my mother knocked harder. After waiting and a few more knocks, she realized the door was slightly ajar and we went in. We walked in and found her friend sitting cross-legged in his living room, his back to us. He didn't move. We walked around. His hands were on his knees and his eyes were closed. We stood there for a moment until he opened his eyes, "Hello," he said, with a big smile. "I was just meditating."

I was unsettled for the rest of the visit. In the car on the way home I asked my mother what meditating meant. "Does meditating mean he didn't hear us knocking?" I wanted to know.

"He could probably hear us," my mom replied. "But it may have been as if we were knocking from very far away."

This answer only made me more unsettled. Was he not there? Was his mind somewhere else? Why did he do that? And how? If a fly landed on his nose, would he feel it? Would it be wrong of him to brush it away? Whatever he was doing, it seemed mysterious and creepy and I wanted nothing to do with it.

I continued to feel that way when I started working for Thay and was told that part of the office culture was to sit for fifteen minutes most mornings. Fifteen minutes seemed like an excruciatingly long time to sit still without anything to read, but I was willing to try it. After all, I was pregnant and tired and sitting down with my eyes closed, even if I had to sit up straight while I did it, seemed like it might actually be a nice rest.

For the last ten years, I have begun most workday mornings like this: My coworkers and I sit in a circle with our eyes closed. We begin the sitting with the ringing of the meditation bell, which is called "inviting the bell" because we're not supposed to "strike" it but rather "invite" it to sound. One person invites the bell, the rest of us just sit with our eyes closed. We just sit. Sometimes the phone rings. Sometimes someone coughs or shifts. I hear it, not as if it was very far away, but just as it is, a cough or a shift. I would like to use this as naptime, since I am often tired in the mornings, but we continue to sit up straight. I used to dislike this aspect of meditation and wondered why I couldn't just lie down. But the sitting encourages my diligence, so that when thoughts come into my mind, it helps me remember to let them come and go, like sticks floating down the river of my consciousness.

When Luna was first born and I'd just come back to work, I craved these first minutes of silence with an addict's intensity. It was the only time of the day that I was awake but not paying attention to someone else or not running around. As my baby got older and I got a little energy back, I started to find that morning meditation close to unbearable. Whole hours would pass in those fifteen minutes. I would feel myself getting older, wasting my life just sitting there like a blob, and I'd begin to panic. I was sure that if I sat for one more minute, I'd die of boredom or old age. I had too much to do. When I finally got everyone out of the house, I wanted to get down to business. The last thing I wanted to do was to sit silently for fifteen endless minutes with the people I work with everyday. I had emails to send, bills to pay, conversations to have, and books to acquire, edit, and send on their way.

The second the meditation was over, all my urgency would evaporate. The email that I was desperate to send a few moments ago could easily wait. Maybe it would be better to review the manuscript a second time before sending it off. I had plenty of time to get a glass of tea and leisurely make my way to my desk.

After ten years of sitting, I no longer either dread or crave that morning meditation. I think of it as not complicated or mysterious, but just an effective way to stop. My mother's friend called it meditation. I just call it quiet, and now I accept it as part of my job description, whether I'm at work or not. I'm only nominally better at letting my thoughts come and go like sticks in the river. I still try and grab the sticks. I can spend the whole of my meditation focusing on whether I can afford to send my kids to summer camp or reviewing what I want to write in a note to an author. The thoughts still feel real; they still feel urgent. But though I still grab at them, I can more quickly let them go until the next stick comes.

The best of stopping and sitting is often the wonderful moment when it is over and I first open my eyes. For that brief first look around, everything feels fresh and clear. This moment makes it worth it, even when the sitting is difficult. Sometimes it comes down to this equation: fifteen minutes of restless sitting for one refreshed, present moment of looking around. For that moment, I'm more available.

It's such a good moment, even if it's short, that I wanted to have this one open-eyed quiet moment with my family, not just with my work colleagues. Now, at dinner each night, our family spends a few quiet minutes together. We invite the bell. Sometimes we close our eyes and sometimes we don't. Usually one of our kids will hum or wiggle around at first. But then they don't. There is a pause, a true silence that feels as precious and full as the sky. Then we open our eyes. We thank the earth and the people whose labors have produced the food. Then we pass the rice and go back to telling stories of the day, making jokes, passing the salt.

That one moment of looking around that we get from stopping, what I call being available, is what Thich Nhat Hanh calls "living in the present moment." The present moment includes what is all around us, both visible and invisible, including the moment's antecedents and descendents. The full awareness of the present moment contains the awareness of every condition, thing, and situation leading up to the moment that made it possible and all the possibilities for the future it contains as well. Being in the present moment doesn't mean we ignore what we know about the past and the future. I don't jump off of cliffs, even if the air is beautiful and the wind inviting, because I think of the moment after. I don't touch hot stoves because I've learned in a past moment that it really hurts. But being in the present moment means that we acknowledge that, even with all that we already know, there is something utterly unique and fresh to the singular moment that we are in right now.

The present moment is a lovely, astonishing place to visit regularly, though hardly anyone lives there full-time. I sometimes think, "I'll be present later" because right now I just have too much else to do. The problem with this is no one knows when the important moments are happening. It's sometimes only late at night when all is quiet and Luna is telling me about the hula hoop game she played at school or about when the man on the street was asking her for food, that I realize these were important moments and not just interruptions. When I'm not being mindful, almost all of life can seem like a series of interruptions of what I thought was important.

Perhaps there will always be moments when I'm only getting from here to there and I'm not that interested in what happens along the way. But as I turned forty, I found that there were too many of those moments in my busy life to ignore them. In his one-man show, *Geezer*, the actor Geoff Hoyle asked, "What happened to the twenty years between the time I was eighteen and twenty-five and the one year between thirty and sixty?" The reason my life has seemed to speed up as I've gotten older is that there were more and more moments when I wasn't available. Enough moments like that in a day and the day is over, without any new thing to remember. Enough days like that, and the week has gone by, then the month, then my life.

When I turned forty and life went from feeling long to feeling short, I began to feel I didn't want to miss a moment more of it. If we're paying attention to each breath, that's a lot of breaths left in our lives until the very end. Life suddenly becomes a lot longer. Some moments will be boring, or painful, or irritating, but if I want to be present for the important satisfying moments, whenever they unexpectedly happen, I need to practice paying attention until attention becomes conscious habit. Researchers of elite athlete and musicians have found that, along with talent and a good memory, it takes ten thousand hours of *deliberate* practice to become really good at something.[*] That's a lot of time practicing conscious awareness of the present moment, just so I can be there for the important moments I can't plan.

There is no way I would have sat for fifteen minutes each morning except that it was part of my work routine. There is no way my kids would be silent for even those few minutes dinner, except that we do it as a family and have for as long as they can remember. Almost every useful and healthy thing I do, from training in martial arts to brushing my teeth, I do because I have made it a conscious habit. If I had to decide to do it each time, I probably wouldn't do it.

Now, when I touch a car door handle, I take a conscious breath. Not because I'm stressed or because I'm trying to be perfectly mindful, but because it makes the car ride go better. When I touch my front doorknob, I do the same. Practicing in these calmer moments helps me remember to check my availability in the less calm moments, when someone is tugging at my sleeve or shouting in my face. I'm in the supermarket or on the street, I move to the side, breathe, and imagine some small child tapping

....
[*] R. J. Duvivier, J. van Dalen, A. M. Muijtjens, V. Moulaert, C. Van der Vleuten, and A. Scherpbier. "The Role of Deliberate Practice in the Acquisition of Clinical Skills," *BMC Medical Education* 11 (2011), 101. The ten thousand-hour theory of deliberate practice was originally formulated by Dr. K. Anders Ericsson, professor of psychology at Florida State University. The role of memory, physiology, family support, coaching, and talent are talked about but not quantified.

my shoulder and asking me if I'm available. I can always say no.

You don't have to be a Buddhist, an anything–ist, or even ever sit still for a long time to be mindful. Many Buddhists throughout the world don't do sitting meditation. But you do need to figure out a way to pause the constant movement and chatter. Any stopping will work, but stopping itself is a requisite condition. Whether we are sitting or standing still or even lying down, when we stop we train our bodies and minds to acknowledge the moment. There are many ways to concentrate the mind during that stopping—counting the breaths, scanning the body, or reciting a small poem are a few ones I've tried—but usually just the intentional stopping is enough. My chattering mind welcomes the opportunity to be free of words. When I do get stuck on words and need to pause the hamster wheel in my head, I use Thay's simple words:

Breathing in, I know I am breathing in.
Breathing out, I know I am breathing out.

Just these few words are often enough to remind me that in my breath, the uniting of body and mind doesn't take effort. It is always there. This present moment is made up, first, of breath. The awareness of the whole universe enters with that inhale and exhale.

7. This Is Why I'm Here

MOST OF THE TIME, I'm not in a controlled environment with a little bell to tell me when to close my eyes and when to open them. Often I'm running around and a lot of that time I'm really not available. A parent at school wants to complain to me about a teacher; my mother calls me at work to tell me that my kids need drum lessons and their pants are too small; or a kid on a bike knocks me over without apologizing. These are the moments when I have no patience or compassion to spare. I'm using the moment to transition from one moment to an imagined future moment and this current moment is just in my way.

Recently, I was speaking with Joanna Macy, a leading environmentalist and author who has written about everything from deep ecology to global peace movements. We were talking about the busyness that everyone we know seems to be stuck in. "After all these years," Joanna said, "the only thing that keeps me from getting lost in a day is setting my intention when I wake up."

After this conversation, I started beginning my mornings by figuring out my intention for that day. Sometimes the whole day's intention can be to take a conscious breath when I get frustrated instead of snapping. Sometimes it's to finish a writing project, listen deeply to one person, or figure out a way to find some joy in the day. Having one intention for that day settles me. It reminds me why I am doing what I'm doing and it allows me to get less stuck in the many other things clamoring for my attention.

Shopping is a clear example. There are so many possible things to buy with so many messages about how they'll improve my life, all clamoring for me to buy them. One day, I stopped on the way to work to get my kids quilts for their beds. They'd been using some old blankets of ours, ripped and so big and weighty that they always ended up on the floor, leaving the kids huddled up and shivering.

I didn't have a lot of time or money so I wanted these things now and cheaply—in the way that sometimes in the United States we've been trained to want and expect things—and so ended up at one of the big box stores designed for that kind of wanting. This all seemed innocuous, but before I realized it, I was hooked on anxiety and old desires.

I didn't know there was such a thing as having rooms where things matched until I went to visit Jennifer Lee's house in fourth grade. Her Hello Kitty bedspread matched her curtains and pillowcases! At the time I assumed this meant that her parents were millionaires. But maybe they just shopped at Target.

Standing in the back corner of the store's second floor, the bright florescent lights glinting off the plastic wrapped around the garish floral and pink polka dot bedspreads, I froze, thinking my kids' well-being and happiness depended on them having a polyester matching quilt and pillow. How could I have failed them up until this point? I was in the "girls" aisle, so everything was flowered and pink. My girls aren't big fans of pink or daisies. There was a "boys" aisle with racecars and rockets on the quilts, but there was no androgynous neutral kid section. The adult section wasn't separated by gender at all. When all those boys and girls grow up, do they all start liking the same gray and maroon bedspreads?

The kid designs were relentlessly cheerful, but they pulled me in. My kids would be thrilled. Perhaps these quilts would help them sleep through the night. Perhaps they would sleep later in the morning! Could I deny them the joy of matching pillows and quilts? Could I stand going into their room and tucking them in under those gigantic polyester daisies? If I didn't get them could I afford the more neutral grown-up ones? I stood there for ten minutes, pacing the boys, girls, and grown-ups aisles. Then I looked at my watch (just as in casinos, there are no clocks in these stores) and realized with relief that I had to go to work and didn't have time to buy anything anyway. As the glass doors closed smoothly behind me, all the urgency was gone and I felt nothing but relief. The sun was shining brightly and my children were fine, with or without the quilts.

꙱

I have found that, even if I set my intention, often I lose it as soon as I get into a car. I'm the least mindful when I'm driving. I can't focus on what needs to happen in front of me and also deal with any other stimulus. City driving is often both numbing and irritating. For a long time after moving back to California from New York, I drove my mom's old car. My mom had been delivering babies for almost forty years and on the back of her car was the bumper sticker "Midwives Help People Out."

Unfortunately, when I drove that car around, my road rage would take over. I would lay on my horn as another car cut in front of me, or yell out the window when someone would try to pass into my lane without seeing me. I had to stop driving so much or get a new car; I was giving midwives a bad name. I did both.

With the exception of my parents and Thay, almost every person I know—from my friend Amalie who works full time at a preschool and then comes home to an immobile husband recovering from surgery, three small children, two dogs, a bearded dragon, and a rabbit; to Tara who is a high-powered lawyer and the executive director of a national nonprofit, has one daughter, and lives with and cares for her elderly parents; to Michael, who runs his own successful tech business, manages a few rental properties, lives alone, and takes violin lessons whenever he can— describes themselves as too busy.

Some people call it scheduling or organizing or transporting or even, optimistically, balancing, but really we are all juggling. Sometimes I think that if I stop and breathe, even if only for a second, everything I need to keep track of will come falling down on my head. But it's not just anxiety or overwork that keeps me from living with full engagement and openness to the present moment. There are the painful moments that I work hard to avoid, and then there is the general way that busyness, rather than mindfulness, becomes my default habit. Paying attention to the present moment doesn't actually take up any extra time. It's just that it's easy to get distracted. This is where intention setting saves me. If I have a clear intention for the day, I get less distracted by a shopping trip that I didn't plan or can't afford, or by my own swirling and urgent emotions.

If I don't set my intention, I use up a lot of my time making many small decisions and figuring out how to triage what I can and can't do and how to fit in what I can. I can fill a whole day making inconsequential decisions, and then, when it comes time to make the big decisions—when I need to figure out how to balance work and family, where I should send my kids to school, how to make our neighborhood safer, and how to get the world going in the direction of more equality, justice, and sustainability—I'm exhausted. It's not just me. "Decision fatigue," as the newspapers and psychologists now call it, means a lot of us end up going with what is easiest, or what is the path of least resistance, or mimicking what others are doing.

Once, after meeting with Thich Nhat Hanh and various monks and nuns, a nun and I took the bus to the airport together. I was curious how they made decisions in the monastery. It must be great, I said, to make decisions in such a peaceful environment where everyone was being compassionate and mindful. Imagine, I thought, no decision fatigue and no rush. She laughed. Imagine, she said, trying to make decisions with five hundred monks and nuns, in over five monasteries in more than three countries, that are trying to act as one body. "It's exhausting," she said, and sometimes it takes months before simple decisions are made. "The difference," she continued, "is not that decision making is easier. It's not. But even if it's messy, we try to find ways to enjoy doing it. The decision making together and with joy is the point, not the final decision."

This makes sense to me because it's how I often deal with physical soreness and pain. I train in kung fu with teenagers who seem to float past as we run our warm-up, while I usually want to stop as soon as the aching starts. Instead, I remind myself, "This is why I'm here." I chose this. Following my intention doesn't necessarily feel good, but it feels better than the alternative. It reminds me to filter all the information and strong emotions coming at me and make a decision that goes along with my purpose. Whether I'm shopping, driving, or running, as long as it's in the service of what I've chosen to be doing, I can be available for it. This is why I'm here.

8. Getting Older Better

I LIKE GOING FAST, whether walking on a street or riding on a rollercoaster. I want to speed things up and get to the good parts rather than slow down. Until I started to really think about aging, I couldn't see the point of focusing on the here and now when there were so many other interesting things to focus on.

Like many people in the United States who make it to forty without serious illness or health problems, I lived the first four decades of my life as if I was invincible. Despite what I saw, despite what I knew thoroughly on a rational level, I didn't imagine myself ever getting older. And while I was aware that it was luck, location, and genes that had kept me mostly healthy, I still somehow suspected that bucking up and not complaining, doing yoga, and eating a regular diet of dark leafy greens would keep me from getting old or sick.

Then, within a few months of turning forty, I got in a bad bicycle accident and tore up my shoulder. I got robbed, got pneumonia, got mostly better, cracked a rib when I was thrown on a hard concrete floor in kung fu, got bronchitis, spent two weeks caring for Jason in the hospital when he developed septic appendicitis, got shingles, and lost a relatively young friend to lung cancer. Not only that, but every bone and muscle in my body felt like it had stopped working properly. My chest hurt every time I sneezed, coughed, or laughed. My bones creaked when I woke up in the morning and when I kneeled down at night, my shoulder ached, and new lines traced grooves into my face while I slept. I tried fish oil, herbs, eating only green leafy vegetables, and a pedicure. Nothing worked.

What was wrong with me? I asked anyone who would listen. The answer was the same, whether it came from my Western doctor, my chiropractor, the Chinese acupuncturist who stuck needles in my ear to help my shoulder, my good friends, or well-meaning strangers on the street: I wasn't simply getting older and better. I was physically beginning to deteriorate.

The physical reality of aging startled me. I always knew it wasn't just a matter of attitude and "you're only as old as you feel." But I figured I had a lot more time before it happened to me. Everyone feels they are becoming old at a different age, but at around forty, our metabolism slows down and our cells really do start to degenerate.*

Of course that doesn't mean that there's nothing we can do. The physical things that we individually have control over that help us live longer and healthier lives are well documented and are the subject of countless books. Current standard advice boils down to this: exercise regularly and eat a healthy, plant-based diet. That's it. Still, no matter how careful we are, no matter where we live, no matter how many miles we run and how much

---

*National Institutes of Health, *Medline Plus*, "Areas of Age-Related Change," Winter 2007, www.nlm.nih.gov/medlineplus/magazine/issues/winter07/articles/winter07pg10-13.html

chlorophyll we munch, our organs can only function for so long. Our cells, even under even the best of circumstances, will degenerate. Even if we avoid tsunamis, cancer, high blood pressure, Bisphenol A in plastics, and falling pianos, we will all age and we will all die.

Although my family history is riddled with several different types of cancer, and my experiences watching my aunt and closest family friend die of breast cancer, I've always planned on a sudden, unexpected death. This was the way, I thought, to separate aging and death a little more. Death, I was hoping, would be unrelated to anything that had come before it. I would still be able-bodied and look pretty much the same as I always have, and then I'd just be gone.

In college, my mother had a boyfriend who told her that, while she wasn't pretty, and certainly wasn't cute, she would be beautiful when she was old. My mother was an Ashkenazi Jew who grew up in Mexico and then lived in New York. She did not fit the traditional ideal of beauty in either place, but while her boyfriend was lacking in tact, he was right about her aging well. She is now strikingly beautiful. Almost daily someone expresses surprise at her age or says wistfully, "I hope I look as good as you do when I'm seventy." She spends a good amount of money on a high-quality facial moisturizer and hair conditioner, but that's about it. She doesn't dye her hair or do any facial injections or peels.

Like my mother, I could never rely on being conventionally beautiful and I do think growing up with little vanity has made aging easier. But despite my resolute lack of interest in mirrors or special creams, aging is a sharp blow to my ego. Somehow, I'd become quite attached to my hair and various other body parts just the way they were. I know everything changes and that impermanence is the one true fact of life, but so soon? Now?

Perhaps it would help if there were some rite-of-passage I could go through: some acknowledgment of crossing the threshold into being old, the way the Jewish Bar Mitzvah, the Mexican Quinceañera, the Greek Dokimasia, or the Catholic First Communion help welcome young people into being fully grown members of their communities. I could consider a huge age-defying physical feat, such as Tamae Watanabe climbing Mount Everest at seventy-three or Diana Nyad attempting a final swim from Cuba to Florida at sixty-one.

But while I could create my own ritual, complete with an arduous mountain climb and a midnight dip in the ocean, I don't want to make it all up myself. I want a ceremony that is as socially understood and acceptable as a wedding—a beautiful, visible sign that I am aging and that, along with my white hair and wrinkles, a new social status is conferred. I want a whole bunch of people who have already crossed over to stand on the shores and show me how it's done.

9. The Height of Engagement

MY LIFE STARTED almost empty of elders. My parents came to California in part to escape their already small East Coast families. All of my grandparents came to the United States and managed to escape pogroms, poverty, and the Holocaust. Most of them died before I was old enough to remember them. On my childhood commune, my parents (who had me at thirty) were considered old. I remember meeting one older gentleman, probably in his seventies as my parents are now, and leaving the encounter profoundly disturbed by the way his skin seemed loose on his body. When I pinched the skin on his hand—I can't imagine now why I did that and why he let me—it stayed lifted where I had pinched it, as if made of a substance separate from the person it covered. Horrified at the idea that this could happen to me, I began the habit of furtively pinching the skin on my hand on my birthday each year, and noting how slowly it returned to its former shape. This is a habit I continue to this day.

Even as an adult, almost all of my older friends are people I've known since childhood. When I lived in New York, I'd occasionally see elderly people walking determinedly down the sidewalk, fighting the wind. On the subway, everyone seemed young. Maybe it was all those stairs. Of course, when I went further uptown I'd see many older New Yorkers, often dressed head to toe in impeccable black, with trim figures and brilliant silver hair elegantly coiffed.

Since moving to the Bay Area, I see even fewer very old people. Partly, this is a function of the lack of public spaces. Everyone is inside more. There are parks, but they seem to be almost entirely full of families with small children. Only when I go into Oakland Chinatown, or Japantown in San Francisco, do I see a hustle and busyness that seems truly intergenerational. When I traveled in Central and South America, Europe, Asia, and North and South Africa, older people were everywhere. I saw them in the plazas in Mexico, I saw them drinking gallons of mint tea in Morocco, riding their bikes in Beijing, out for early morning walks in Tuscany. In each place, babies and teenagers and grown-ups and elders were all jumbled together.

As a thirteen-year-old, I visited Nicaragua for a month with other U.S. teenagers and I remember being surprised by the teenagers there—how responsible they seemed, how interested in conversing with adults and able to connect to and affect the events around them. Many of them credited their grandparents and other elders in their community for inspiring them. A friend who grew up in Iran also commented on the particular isolation of American youth. Where he grew up, the end of youth was the army; it came on so quickly that it lent a seriousness to adolescence. Here, there is no fixed end to youth. For some, it ends with having children; for others, when they begin to take care of someone else or with the responsibility of work. Others seem to go straight from youth to old age.

When I was thirty, I ended up leading a group of elders to South Africa on a two-week history tour. I'd never been to South Africa, but I'd read a lot and felt pretty confident until I arrived at the airport and saw that all the tour participants, with the exception of one person, were well over seventy and that two of the men were in their mid-nineties. They were all cheerful, knowledgeable, and excited. The two nonagenarians had notes from their doctors saying they were healthy and fit to travel. What could go wrong?

One man had a heart attack and another had heart failure. One spent the majority of the trip in the hospital but recovered completely. The group carried on, as we made it past the lions and giraffes on the safari, through the shantytowns, to the hospital and back to visit our friends, and into the remote Western Cape. We changed our itinerary as we went, making more bathroom stops and shorter trips.

That was over ten years ago. Until I started to realize that I was getting on the other side of old, I hadn't also realized that the friends and teachers around me were also getting old. When I look around at Joanna Macy and Thich Nhat Hanh, my nonagenarian friends Cynthia and Millie, my parents, my children, and the families in our community, I know that our time when we are all alive together is limited. Thich Nhat Hanh has clear skin, bright eyes, and the energy to go for long walks each morning, teach, and then garden in the afternoon. My parents, in their seventies, have more energy and activities planned than I do. My father, Osha, has two kinds of cancer, a degenerating nerve disease, and a host of smaller ailments. Yet he runs around all day painting, writing, lawyering, and carrying signs at every protest both large and small. My mother, Yeshi, is always on her way to one adventure or another, working as a health educator in the Ecuadorian jungle, then coming back to the states to deliver a few babies, go on a silent retreat, teach a leadership seminar, and counsel families of newborns on everything from communication to lactation. Millie still exercises every day and takes care of her grandchildren and great-grandchildren. Cynthia, until her recent death, ran her home like a community center and artists' think tank. It wasn't that my elders didn't have the aches and difficulties of old age, it's just that they were so busy, I hadn't noticed their aging.

That doesn't mean that their aging isn't without loss and sorrow. Osha wishes he could still ride a bicycle and weld. Thay suggests we walk wherever we can, because one day our legs will be too weak to walk. He admits,

I suffer from old age and I practice a lot with that suffering. It used to be that my memory was very good. Whenever I wanted a word whether in English, or French, or Vietnamese, that word would jump up. But the other day, at two o'clock in the morning, I forgot a word and I couldn't sleep after that. I turned on the light and pulled out all my dictionaries in order to find that word. I got out so many dictionaries because I was angry and I couldn't accept the fact that I was old. That word was "saltpeter." "Saltpeter" is a kind of salt that grows on old things. I wanted that word and I couldn't get it. Everybody was sleeping. There was no one to ask. When I opened the dictionary I didn't even know the word started with an "s."

One time I tried to remember the name of Charles Darwin. I was sitting on the bus and I was thinking about Darwin, and I couldn't remember his name. I couldn't bear it that I couldn't remember. But I have to accept that every day there are cells in my brain that are dying. My resistance against my old age is just foolishness; it's not wisdom. Wisdom is accepting that we are old and wisdom is also seeing that we are not old. We are equally a part of the new baby letting out its first yelp and the young daffodil rising up to the light.*

A few years later, Thay told me, "For me, aging has become a joy. It's a chance to be in the smooth part of the river, not rushing to the sea. I get to go slow enough to savor and reflect the clouds and the birds going by." Osha says, "I've lost physical ability and some memory but I've also gained freedom from anxiety, obsession, and fear. It's an exhilarating time." Yeshi is

* Thich Nhat Hanh in a Dharma talk given 7 July, 1996.

enjoying herself more fully than ever before, giving herself per-
mission to do all the things that she wasn't able to as a single
working mother.

Yeshi, Osha, and Thich Nhat Hanh had completely different lifestyles. They each eat different things, believe in different
things, and are in various stages of health, illness, and wealth. But
they all seem at the height of engagement with their lives and,
at least in the case of my parents, more joyful and relaxed than
when they were in their thirties and forties. In fact, they seem a
lot happier and more at ease than most of the younger grown-ups
I know. I have been "aging" in ways that I can no longer ignore,
but these teachers reminded me that part of that aging is having
the tools and resources to engage fully with my life. Their lives
are a contradiction to the idea of our youth-focused culture that
old age and irrelevance increase in equal proportion. I know that
there will likely be some slowing down as I grow older, as well as
more aches and more pain ahead, but these teachers remind me
that a potential deep joy awaits me as well.

10. Tomorrow Is Not the Answer

UNLIKE ME, both my daughters are very excited about getting older. The biggest compliment you can give Plum, who is four, is to tell her she's acting like a seven-year-old. Luna, who is nine, prefers to be told she seems like a teenager, but not, as she puts it, "the sassy kind." They have big dreams for what will happen when they are grown-up, including being famous scientist bakers together. Plum thinks that she'll no longer suck her thumb and that she'll have yogurt with maple syrup for breakfast, lunch, and dinner. Luna imagines being able to read for hours and hours at night, with no one ever telling her it's time to turn out the light. One day, far in the future, they want to walk to the ice cream store by themselves. Both of them find adulthood impossible to imagine. They love to talk about how one day they'll each be one hundred years old and still, as they both reassure me, living with me at home.

I remember the day I decided that I didn't want to get any older. I was sixteen. Life was not great. I was insecure and shy, with the doomed triple combination of braces, glasses, and pimples. We had no money and there was a lot of yelling about that. My stepmother was unkind, my father ineffectual and busy, and my mother distracted. School was boring, except at lunchtime, when it was terrifying. My best friend had recently ditched me for a new best friend while I was in the bathroom stall. We'd gone in the bathroom together and then, while I was in the next stall, she'd run out and hid with her new friend behind the math building. The next day, she slipped a "Dear Jane" note in my locker, saying our friendship was over. She'd gotten "cooler," she explained, while I, unfortunately, had not.

But while I wasn't cool, my body was strong and lean and I loved being in it. I loved debating in history class, doodling in chemistry class, writing short stories, and thinking I knew it all. I loved feeling "old for my age" because I could win arguments with grown-ups. I had kissed a boy and was relieved to have it over with. I loved the sense that the world was open in front of me and I was now old enough to take advantage of it. I was still debating whether to be president or a rock star. Every adventure, every destination seemed possible.

For the first time, I no longer waited eagerly for my birthday. I didn't want to get older, but I was growing older, and from now on, that was the way it was going to be. I wanted to do the things older people got to do—go to clubs, vote, get my own car—but I didn't want to have to be older to do them. My dad was a muralist and my mother was a midwife, and their friends were artists, politicians, and teachers. But while the grown-ups I knew were unconventional, energetic, and creative, it was clear that they weren't young people. They got tired. They needed a lot of sleep. They were afraid of flying in hot air balloons and jumping off of high rocks. They didn't eat candy.

Most days, I dreamed of escaping on an ocean liner to Paris, my short hair dyed bright red. I'd carry nothing but a leather bag filled with a journal, two silk dresses, and two pairs of underwear. I'd wear one dress and pair of underwear one day, then wash them and switch. I made a deal with the movie director in the sky I'd always imagined in place of a god: I would be good and kind as long as I got to stay sixteen forever or maybe get as old as nineteen, but that was it. Any older was nonnegotiable.

My children think that as an adult I have so many choices. I get to pick the important things, like how much sugar they can have, if they're sick enough to stay home from school, and when it's time to go to bed. They see that as they get older, they get to make more choices and they have more responsibility. But the balance hasn't tipped yet. The choices are still mostly fun, their responsibilities minor. They cannot imagine this part of growing older: where the responsibilities weigh heavier than the choices and where physical exhaustion does not end because someone picks you up and carries you to bed, tucking you in with a kiss.

I don't idealize childhood. At times it was confusing and terrifying and without solace. But I do miss that time when getting older seemed like the solution to everything. I miss the part of thinking I was only getting older because I wanted to so desperately and that I could stop whenever I wanted.

Now I know there is no magic solution on the horizon. I can't just wait until next year and then everything will be different and better. Next year I won't be bigger than the mean kids and be able to reach the highest rung on the monkey bars. I have to stop waiting for things to happen. If I want to reach the top monkey bar, I have to start reaching for it now, or at least give it my best try.

One of the advantages of stopping and spending more time in the present moment is that I have become more aware that there are only present moments ahead of me—and fewer of them than there used to be. Thich Nhat Hanh has told me he thinks old age is delicious. My parents say these years are the most peaceful and the most interesting. I hope I feel like that when I am their age. But I am not counting on it. I'm going for more peace right now. I'm being pulled along by that river rushing to the sea; at least I'm learning to enjoy the rush.

PART II
Engaged

11. Attack and Paddle

AFTER MY FAMILY LEFT the mountain commune, we returned every summer, sleeping in tents and building a cabin with friends on a lush flat of land beside the Salmon River in Northern California. The year I turned ten, the first year the Salmon had ever been rafted, my mother decided we should raft it. We went with our family friend Wally, a house builder, champion fisherman, and experienced river guide. Wally had a solid build and an impressive handlebar mustache that wiggled as he explained two key river safety guidelines: First, left and right were always "River Left" and "River Right" if you were facing downriver. Second, we should never stand up in fast-moving shallow water. If we did, he explained, we could get our foot caught between rocks and get pulled under. If that happened, Wally said, "You just turned something that wasn't a problem, into a problem."

We were in two boats. Wally, a few family friends, and my mom were in one boat. I was in the other boat with my friend, her mom, and Wally's son, a junior river guide. Since our boat had the kids in it and the other boat had Wally, Wally's boat went first. We were supposed to follow once he had figured out the safest route.

The river was wild, exhilarating, and terrifying. When we hit the rapids, I often held back, frozen, gripping the paddle as if it were a lifesaver, but not using it. But when the river was just pulling us along, I loved it. We dipped in and out of eddies, and lightly bounced off underwater boulders. We pointed out circling hawks, the beautiful oxidized patterns in the rocks, and the manzanita and pine saplings that seemed to grow out of sheer granite cliffs. In one calm stretch, a shiny brown river otter swam alongside us, its head like a small wet coconut.

Then we reached Freight Train, a long, bumpy rapid I'd often stared at from the road up above. As planned, Wally's boat entered the rapid ahead of us. As we watched, we saw Wally fly out of the boat, disappearing under the rushing whitewater. The rapid was pulling our raft down; there was no time to pull out to the side. Wally's wet gray head popped up, "Attack and paddle," he yelled to us. "Attack and paddle!"

Wally had explained to us earlier that attack and paddle, rather than freeze, is the only way to survive a rapid. If you hold back, lean away, and try to enter it as little as possible, your boat is more likely to flip and the rapid gains control. You have to lean into it. We'd all nodded when he'd explained this before we'd gotten into the rafts, but at the time, my friend and I were more interested in comparing the stripes on our new blue and white bathing suits.

Now, with the cold water splashing into our folded raft, I leaned forward and paddled for all I was worth. We went right into the belly of the rapid and it carried us through, fast and smooth, just as it was supposed to. It was one of the most joyful and liberating rides of my life. I was fully engaged and available to the moment.

∞

There are many times when I don't want to be available. It's not just that I'm busy, I just don't want this particular moment and I'd rather not have a full-body engaged awareness of it. Being aware and open leads to feeling pain, and sometimes the idea of adding new pain is enough to make me want to detach completely and go off and live alone in a hut made of sticks on a mountaintop.

Mindfulness isn't about choosing to just be more aware of the pleasant or happy moments. It requires the full-body slam of the hard times, the complicated times, and the painful times. For these moments, just as when I'm physically hit in kung fu, breathing helps. We can't choose whether or not there are going to be rapids. We're going to get soaked whether we paddle or not, but the more engaged we are, the more our awareness deepens our connection to life instead of pulling us away from it. And when we're more connected, we suffer less.

But there is no way to be fully engaged in the world and not feel a lot of pain. There are the unexpected sharp pains and then there is the exhaustion of chronic pain. There is physical pain and there is the emotional suffering that I add to it with my judgment, sadness, and anger. And there is the emotional suffering that comes from my relationships and my awareness of the suffering of others. I walk around with all of this.

I had always imagined myself having one daughter. The details (a partner or no partner, more kids or just one) were fuzzy, but I knew I wanted that. It took me years to get pregnant with Luna and after we had her, I was too busy working and taking care of her to think about having another child. Then, when Luna was a few months shy of three, I found out I was pregnant. Jason and I were more surprised than two people who know how babies are made had any right to be. We talked for hours about whether or not to have this child. There was no good reason, as my father said, to have another baby. The world didn't need more kids and Luna had plenty of other kids to play with. That was all true, but having babies is not usually a rational decision and this one was growing inside me. I wanted to name it Grace.

My mother, some family friends, and Luna and I went to stay in the home of a family friend in Mexico. It was, I thought, a chance to be alone with Luna before this new child was born. Driving from our friend's home back to the airport, I started bleeding. By the time we arrived at the airport, I was bent over with cramping pain and bleeding heavily. Flight attendants settled me into a wheelchair and then wheeled me on to the plane.

As soon as the plane lifted off, the pain got worse. I could barely see. I locked myself in the bathroom, needing privacy and a place to clean up some of the blood. The toilet made a loud sucking sound when I flushed. There, in the airplane bath-room, this small thing, a clump of bloody tissue, came out into my hands.

In almost every one of his books, Thay talks about the con-cept of continuation. Like the wave in the ocean or the cloud in the sky, we don't really have a beginning or an ending; we merely change forms and continue. In that cramped airplane bathroom, flying from Puerto Vallarta to San Francisco, this started to feel deeply true. Life does not begin or end with con-ception. Life continues always and we dip in and out. At nine weeks, a zygote is a soft egg sack no bigger than my palm. It is an idea named Grace.

I wrapped the clump in a napkin and went back to my seat. I took the four ibuprofen my mother handed me. I carried the clump through customs in that napkin. As they wheeled me in a wheelchair through the airport, I thought, "Nobody better dare mess with me." When I got home, I put the balled-up napkin in the refrigerator and fell asleep on the floor.

A week later, I woke up in my own bed. It was night. It was raining. Jason and my mother were there. We went out to the garden and I pressed the shovel into the earth. I pulled out thick clods of dirt. I dug a hole in the wet earth and placed the clump of tissue inside. I sang to myself as I dug. Upstairs, my three-year-old daughter slept with the window open, the rain coming in. This is the song I sang: Life begins now. Life begins right now.

ༀ

The Chinese character for "forbearance" has two parts. One part signifies the heart, and the other part represents a sharp knife. The heart is so big that even the knife can't destroy it. The Buddha used the image of a glass of dirty water. The dirt makes the glass of water undrinkable. But if you were to empty the glass into a large, fresh river, you could drink from the river. The river is so big, it can easily absorb the dirt. I find this image comforting. There is pain in the river. But there are a lot of other things in it, too. It's cold, and full of leaves and soil and living creatures. Swimming in it, the pain slides past, comes again, and slides past. When I emerge, I am shivering but I know that I am all right.

One of the Buddhist concepts I have struggled with the most is "nonattachment." It's our attachment to our views and perceptions, Thich Nhat Hanh writes, that bring us and others so much suffering: "Attachment to views is the foundation for exclusion, fear, anger, craving, and despair. If you are truly practicing Right View, there is no room for these sufferings."*

I like a lot of my views and so I have found this difficult to accept. My perceptions and beloveds give me pleasure, even if it is my attachments that have also brought me the most pain. The most wonderful and difficult moments of my life have come when I am fully engaged, every cell fully committed and "attached." I treasure those moments.

....
*Thich Nhat Hanh, *Good Citizens: Creating Enlightened Society* (Berkeley, CA: Parallax Press, 2012).

But the attachment that Thay talks about here is a clinging to our views, not an openness to life. It's the clinging to my certainties (this idea named Grace that is buried in my yard, this idea that I will never have another child, this idea that my uncertainty about having this child is what kept it from growing into one) that keeps me from being fully open and engaged in the moment. Full attachment, as I want to live it, is the opposite of clinging. Full attachment involves two elements: not waiting for life to happen and not holding back from the fullness of life—the challenges and suffering as well as the joy.

The elders who I consider my teachers have only become more engaged as they get older, rather than more detached. Perhaps this is a fuller awareness of the reality and inevitability of death. There is no more saving our energy for later, the way I was unconsciously doing on the beginning of our raft trip. Whatever pain they have had, and I know there has been plenty, has kept them moving toward life, rather than away from it. I think of my mother, Yeshi, always the last one to leave the dance floor, with the younger people sitting exhausted on the sidelines and then her returning home, alone. I think of Osha, my father, hanging out under the railroad tracks with his homeless clients at ten o'clock at night, crumpling and crying when the exhaustion hits him, but not pushing anything away. And I think of Thay, resting and fanning himself in his hammock, enjoying the swaying back and forth and the shifting light, as we talk about possible book ideas for the coming year.

12. Pain and Practice

EVEN THE HEALTHIEST and most pain-free among us, if we are lucky enough to live long enough to be old, will experience some kind of daily physical pain. The body does not go gently. Pain, both emotional and physical, is unavoidable. But that doesn't stop me from trying to outwit it. It's like a shot; the anticipation is often much worse than the moment itself. It's the suffering, the fear, and the loneliness, that I fear more.

In the Puttamansa Sutra, the Buddha tells the story of the second arrow. Pain, both physical and emotional, is an arrow that hits its mark. But, the Sutra says, "if a second arrow strikes a person at that very same spot, the pain will be much more than doubled. If a third arrow strikes in that same spot, then again, the pain will be a thousand times more intense."[*] We may have a strong desire to make pain go away, a fear that it will never leave, or anxiety about what it means. A second arrow, striking in the same spot as the first, hurts more than twice as much. Sister Dang Nghiem, a nun I work with, put it like this: "If you have pain or discomfort in your body, stop and embrace it. Know this pain is not 'you.' You can be there for your pain without becoming the pain.[**]

----
[*] Thich Nhat Hanh, *Old Path White Clouds* (Berkeley, CA: Parallax Press, 1991).
[**] Sister Dang Nghiem, *Healing* (Berkeley, CA: Parallax Press, 2010).

When my second daughter, Plum, was born, I had been editing Buddhist teachers for four years. She was born in our bedroom on a clear October afternoon notable for the unrelenting blueness of the sky and my strong craving for chicken sandwiches throughout the labor. She was delivered into Jason's arms. The only other people there were her sister Luna, my parents, and one good family friend. Unlike Luna's birth, which involved over fifty hours of labor, intravenous antibiotics, an epidural, three doctors, and four midwives, Plum's birth was relatively short and easy. But twelve hours later, she developed a fever and we rushed to the Neonatal Intensive Care Unit at the local Children's Hospital.

No one at the hospital could figure out what was wrong with her, and that particular day no one was in the mood to be very gentle about it. They poked and prodded her, ordering a spinal tap, a chest x-ray, and vial after vial of blood. We had come in the early afternoon, but the clock in the windowless room showed that it was now night. The attending doctor, brisk and irritated by her long shift, spoke. Meningitis. Deformed internal organs. Brain infection. I drowned out her words by humming Plum a lullaby. "You shouldn't sing 'You are my *only* sunshine' to your kid," the doctor snapped at me. "Especially if you have another kid at home. It makes your child think she's special."

Outside, a man and a woman yelled at each other. There was a loud thud against our door, a body being slammed. A cry of pain. Another nurse came in. "The police are on their way to take care of that situation," he said.

They put us in a tiny room within the NICU designed for babies that were dangerously contagious. There was a fan constantly whirring, sucking away germs we couldn't see. A large, noisy clock on the wall ticked away the seconds. Twenty-four hours passed while we waited for test results. The lights never went out, the monitors never stopped beeping, and Plum alternately slept and cried. We brought in a folding picnic chair and Jason and I took turns sleeping in it next to her. Plum's fever went down and she nursed. They said we could go home. Then, they told us they'd made a mistake. Plum had a staph infection and had to stay. Another twenty-four hours passed without day or night. Then, they told us that the sample was contaminated, Plum didn't have staph, and they needed to draw more blood. If the blood was clean, they assured us, she could go home the next morning.

Her third and final night in the hospital, Jason went home to sleep and my friend Geba kept me company. I sat in our picnic chair, holding Plum, encouraging her to nurse, and Geba curled up on the tiny, infant-size foam mattress. After a few hours, we switched positions, and Geba held Plum while I curled up. We stayed like this all night; staring at the clock and watching the seconds tick, counting them down till the morning when we'd be allowed to leave. This night, though, the seconds didn't count down. At two in the morning, daylight savings time ended. As we watched the clock, it started moving backward. In a few minutes, it was one again. We had to relive that same hour again, second by second.

There were many places I wanted to be that night, but the present moment was not one of them. The present moment felt endless and painful. I listened to songs by monks and nuns from Thich Nhat Hanh's tradition, but in the hopes of being distracted from the moment, not returning to it. Finally, as the clock showed two in the morning for the second time, I made my peace. I was able to notice, as Thay says, the conditions for happiness in that moment. Everything was not okay, but some things were. I could breathe easily. I was holding my daughter in my arms and she was alive and warm and breathing well. Not all the parents in the NICU could say that. My body ached and I was still bleeding from the birth, but my senses were working, and I was fine. I was with loved ones, including my child and an adult who had known me since birth. I felt calm, ridiculously lucky, humbled, and grateful. I thought of the other babies in their little glass cubes. I fell asleep hunched over in the chair, Plum in my arms. I woke to a nurse shaking me. It was morning. I had slept for an hour. We were going home. We packed up our chair, our soiled clothes, and the various odds and ends of our stay. On the way out, I met the eyes of a father coming to visit his child in the NICU. We held each other's gaze, neither of us attempting a smile.

Although there are all kinds of Buddhists with all kinds of beliefs, most of them begin with the Buddha's first teaching, the

talk he gave to his close friends soon after finding enlighten-
ment under the Bodhi tree. There are Four Noble Truths, he told
them, and they can be boiled down to this: 1. Life is suffering. 2.
Attachment is the cause of our suffering. 3. There is a way out of
suffering. 4. The way out of suffering is to follow the Eightfold
Path of Right View, Right Thought, Right Speech, Right
Action, Right Intention, Right Livelihood, Right Diligence,
Right Concentration, and Right Mindfulness.

I first read these teachings years ago on the painted wall of
a restaurant in downtown Berkeley. At the time they seemed to
be saying that the way to be happy was to distance myself from
all wants, worries, and desires, and to do everything right, which
seemed unlikely.

But I don't think that's what the Four Noble Truths mean.
I have found in my own suffering that the seeds of compassion,
for myself and others, are there, but only if I acknowledge the
suffering in the first place.

Thay says, "Our natural tendency is to try to run away
from suffering. This has become a collective habit. We medi-
cate ourselves with alcohol, drugs, sedatives, and tranquilizers to
get away from our suffering. But the First Noble Truth suggests
that we should stay and acknowledge our suffering. If we don't
understand suffering, we can't understand happiness either. My
definition of heaven is a place where there is plenty of understanding and compassion, and that implies that suffering is there.
If there's no suffering, then it's not a very good place to learn."[*]

If happiness was all that mattered, I would be set. Because the conditions of happiness are always right in front of me. I can, at any given moment, notice that my teeth don't hurt, that the sky has a patch of brilliant blue, or that the air smells clean. I don't have to wait until these things are gone—until I have a toothache or it's dark and stinky outside—to appreciate them. These are small things. But there are also large wonderful things going on all the time: new life, whole forests and mountains and oceans, human beings being brave and loving, the mystery and beauty of orangutans and red-bellied frogs.

The conditions of suffering are always right in front of me as well, both my own personal suffering and the suffering of others. Some of this suffering is large-scale human suffering: exploitation, executions, starvation, dictatorships, and wars that are going on all over the planet. Then there is the large and small suffering of our individual lives: We don't get what we want; someone doesn't invite us somewhere; our bodies break down and hurt; people abandon or betray us. Everyone we love leaves, ages, and dies.

ೲ

I am standing across from my kung fu teacher, waiting for her to punch me. My shoulders are tense, and I hunch slightly, dreading

*Thich Nhat Hanh, *Good Citizens: Creating Enlightened Society* (Berkeley, CA: Parallax Press, 2012).

the punch, even though I know I can and will block it. My teacher puts her arms down. She looks at my tight shoulders and shakes her head. "You're going to get hit," she said. "But that doesn't mean you're going to get injured. Getting hit is inevitable. It might hurt, but you'll be fine. The sooner you accept that, the sooner you can relax and block the punch." My shoulders dropped. I hadn't realized how afraid I'd been. Fear was making me tense; it wasn't keeping me safe.

If I accept that I'm going to be hit, that I'm going to experience pain, sorrow, and fear, two things happen. First, I'm less likely to shoot myself with the second arrow, the arrow of anxiety and worry. Second, I relax and am more open to happiness. It's not a balance sheet, where the suffering and the happiness equal each other out. They don't. But mindfulness has taught me that they are both there when we fully engage with our lives. Thich Nhat Hanh reminds me, "To learn the art of creating happiness and to learn the art of handling our suffering are the same thing."

When I first held my two daughters, I felt there was nothing I wouldn't do to save them from suffering. I learned pretty quickly, with the first fever, that they would suffer. Some of that suffering is not only inevitable, it will become the source of their physical and emotional strength and their compassion. But it's also true that life is filled with so much *unnecessary* suffering. Some of this unnecessary suffering, such as hunger, poverty, and violence, has injustice as its root cause. Other kinds of suffering, the suffering that we cling to, is the suffering that comes from our perceptions and views and fills us up with anxiety, worry, anger, and guilt. This is the suffering that gets in the way of awareness. When I look at it this way, my attachment to my experience isn't the problem, it is my attachment to control, my desire to not just enjoy my views but insist on them, and the misperception that happiness depends on any one material or physical thing.

Mindful awareness will never make me as sedate and calm as others seem to be. I'm not looking to forgo dancing, shouting, loud laughter, and crying. But mindful awareness of the pain when it comes, and the steady constant inhale and exhale of my breath, makes the pain bearable. Thich Nhat Hanh advises me, "Walk like a free person. Put things down, don't carry anything, and you will feel light." I don't think there is any conflict between the Buddhist ideal of nonattachment to views as the way out of suffering and my own adherence to "attack and paddle" full engagement, as long as that full engagement has lightness in it. When the pain and pleasure come, the less I'm clinging, the more agiley I can ride the rapid. My joy will pass, just as my suffering does, and I will remain in the river, breathing, as the moments come one right after the other.

13. Permission to Cry

IF I WANT TO "walk like a free person" without the old pain following me, I have to let the pain come when it comes, and then let it go. Maybe I just say this because I'm a big crier. My kids say they have only seen me cry once each, but that seems impossible. I cry all the time, at everything from injustice, exploitation, poverty, disease, and hunger, to sappy movies and a well-written sentence. I cry when I hurt myself. I cry when other people hurt themselves. I cry when I see people being very brave. I cry when I think about my kids becoming teenagers and the stupid risks they'll take. I cry when I think about my children learning the details of human history, our capacity for genocide, enslavement, and cruelty. I cry when I think about dying. I'm good in a crisis, able to think and take charge and do what needs to be done. But as soon as it's over, I break down and wail.

I'm not a dainty, quiet crier, either. Sometimes there's the single subtle tear, but more often I'm given to the gut-wrenching, full-body sobs that make my nose stuffy and my eyes red. Given all that, it's odd that my kids have so rarely seen those tears.

I tell them that I like to cry in private, since crying usually feels like a private thing. I'd also rather my kids didn't think they had to take care of me while they're still kids. The time Luna saw me cry was a couple of years ago. We were walking down our stairs and I fell and twisted my knee. It was a sharp, twisting kind of pain and for a little while I couldn't get up so I sat there and cried. My knee is fine, but Luna still talks about it to this day.

The time Plum saw me cry was last week. My mother and I had had a big fight, a rare enough thing that it left aftershocks. Later, as Plum and I were lying on the couch looking at a book, she said, "Mama, I never saw you cry before."

"Really?" I asked. "How was it for you? What did you think?"

"It wasn't good and it wasn't bad," she said. "It just was."

∽

After many of the talks that Thay gives, there is a question and answer session. When I was new to editing, I faithfully transcribed the answers to these sessions. I didn't want to miss something that would be a good addition to a book I was working on. But as I reviewed my scribbled notes, I found that, with an exception or two each time, people asked the same questions. No matter what the talk was about, invariably one of the first questions someone would ask is: What should I do about a particularly strong emotion—be it anger, sadness, fear, attraction, or jealousy? Just having the feeling is so strong, so seemingly unbearable, that all we want to know is what to *do* with it so we can have some relief. Thay's response to these questions is invariably almost identical to Plum's. There's nothing to do with the emotion. It just is. We can be gentle with it, breathe with it, and not hold it too tightly. Perhaps, if we are ready, we can seek to understand it and look at its roots. This is secondary. The critical first step is to acknowledge it.

Thay's book *Happiness* sums it up: "A strong emotion is similar to a storm, and it can create a lot of damage. We need to figure out a way to protect ourselves, to create a safe environment, and to wait out the storm. We cannot sit and wait for the storm to go by quickly while we receive all the damage of the storm directly. Keeping our body and mind safe from the storm is our practice. We go to the trunk of a steady tree and ride out the storm. After each storm, we become stronger, more solid, and soon we're no longer fearful of storms. We no longer pray for a calm sky and a calm ocean. Instead, we pray that we have the wisdom and strength to deal with the difficulties that arise."[*]

This definition of strong emotions makes intuitive sense to Plum. While Luna turns inward when she is sad or angry, Plum becomes a whirling raging storm, ready to smash the world to smithereens. She plots the death of all her family members in great detail. She disowns us. She walks out the front door and gets about halfway down the block. Then she just stands there, frozen and furious. As soon as the emotion passes, she is calm and smiling, eyes bright, ready to hug and to help. It has been a great lesson to watch a storm unfurl and to know there is absolutely nothing I can do to stop it once it has begun to unfurl. I

[*] Thich Nhat Hanh, *Happiness: Essential Mindfulness Practices* (Berkeley, CA: Parallax Press, 2009).

remember what Thay says about not praying for calm weather. I don't try to avoid the tantrums by placating her. Rather, if they come, they come. I cultivate the habits of stopping, sitting, and conscious breathing each day so that when the storm comes I can reflexively find refuge in conscious breathing until it passes.

While they express strong emotions very differently, both Luna's collapse and Plum's hurricane often end in tears. I see them cry at least every week, if not every other day. Like their mama, they are serious criers. They cry over messed-up drawings, a snatched doll, a withheld treat, toothpaste on their pajamas, a stubbed toe, a dead butterfly, and such a myriad of other small and large reasons that I could not begin to list them all. Jason and I have to regularly remind ourselves that their crying is totally fine, even if it can be irritating. It doesn't mean we have to try to fix the problem or change our own behavior. In other words, crying doesn't usually get you the thing you felt you needed, but it can help you release the feeling that you will die without it.

To Plum at least, my crying was no different. I was upset so I cried and then I was done and I was okay. She didn't expect that she had to do anything about it or that it meant more than it was. Some things just are. We can cry, we can acknowledge all the many things that are wrong, and then we fix what we can fix and move on.

14. How Do You Know?

ONE OF THE REASONS I'm so attached to my attachments is that for me full attachment has been hard won. I come from a long line of worriers and questioners and we rarely accept the fullness of the present moment without a fight, a question, and an escape route.

This has its advantages. It keeps us skeptical so we don't often get stuck in the kind of attachment to views that can lead to dogmatism or fanaticism. In my family, the questioning starts early, as it does with most kids, but it's not a phase that has an end. At three-and-three-quarters, Plum had to know the age of every person she saw. If she saw another three-year-old, she had to know if that child was "plain three," or if not, how many quarters were involved. As Plum was determined to get big and old as soon as possible, she was pleased to point out those that were younger than she was.

"Everybody is older than somebody and younger than somebody," I would say reassuringly. "Yes," she would answer, not appeased. "But, I'm younger than most people in the whole world." It was true. Plum carried her relative youth as a terrible burden, not just at home, where she could not escape being the youngest person, but even in our neighborhood and in the entire universe.

One day, when I was picking her up from preschool, she wanted to know the exact age of her friend Serena, who was having a birthday in a couple of weeks. I told her Serena was two-and-three-quarters.

"Two-and-three-quarters?" Plum said incredulously. "Is that even a number?"

"Yes," I tell her. "It is."

"But how do you know?" she asked.

That's a good question and one that I find myself often unable to answer clearly. I haven't done any independent hands-on research into the subject. But telling her that I know something is true because people have told me it's true doesn't really go with the whole idea I'm trying to teach her about questioning views and how there's a diffuse border between the subject (the thinker) and the object (the thing they are thinking about). I'm constantly reminding Plum and Luna to figure things out for themselves and not just believe what other people tell them. So why don't I take my own advice?

A little while later, driving home, we passed a couple of kids, who looked around ten- or eleven-years-old, walking down the street. Plum wanted to know where their mama was. I told her that when you reach that age, sometimes you can walk home by yourself, with no mama.

"But how do you know?" she asked.

I don't know why I think, for this neighborhood, for this time of day, ten is a reasonable age to walk home alone. There are so many factors that go into that decision and no right answer.

The question of how I know things comes up several times a day. How do I know our car won't crash? How do I know that koalas are real? How do I know that guns kill people? Have I ever seen one kill someone? How do I know that the turkey at the Little Farm won't eat her shoes? I wish she would ask me an easy question, like how do I know stoves are hot, and I could answer her with a story based on my own experience, but she already knows about stoves. What she wants to know is how we've reached consensus on the other stuff and how we've made the parameters of consensual reality that she's discovering is the world. I almost never come up with an answer that satisfies either of us, but at least I'm reminded to ask the question.

15. Worrying and Breathing

QUESTIONING KEEPS ME from getting stuck in my views, but often the questioning in our house turns into worrying. My eldest daughter, Luna, is a worrier. She worries about the door being closed all the way, about people dying or not picking her up on time. She worries about which plants are poisonous and which ones aren't, about litter on the streets, and people fighting. She's worried that segregation will come back and she will not be able to sit next to her friends and that there are places where children are killed by earthquakes and tsunamis. She worries that people get put in jail too much and that it makes them meaner. She's not afraid of monsters, pirates, or dragons. For the most part, she worries about real things that might actually happen.

Each summer my family spends five weeks in the mountains, in a small cabin with no electricity inside and bears outside. The river is cold and full of rapids that Luna loves to swim in. We're far off the grid and the worries seem to fade there, though they do try to sneak in sometimes at night. But as soon as we're back in the city, the worries are waiting for her.

Luna's strong and smart, and the worries don't always win. They don't keep her from enjoying school or from making friends and playing with them. They don't keep her from loving swimming, climbing, and cooking. But they keep her from enjoying herself as much as she could and sometimes they keep her up at night. One night she asked me if there was such thing as a "worrying disease" and if she had it.

Adults often talk about anxiety as something diagnosable and manageable—not necessarily curable, but manageable with some combination of therapy and possibly medication. Anxiety, the doctors say, is often genetic. It runs in a family, like depression. Luna comes from a long line of worriers. My sister was terrified of chicken pox, breast cancer, and unlocked doors. My aunt worried each day that she wasn't liked or beautiful and that she would die of breast cancer. When the cancer did finally kill her, thousands came to talk of how much they loved her. My father struggled with obsession and anxiety until he reached his seventies.

I know that worrying doesn't "help" and it doesn't seem necessarily "healthy" but it certainly seems natural. I can see why worry evolved in human beings—to help us distinguish between safe and poisonous plants and to help us figure out a way to avoid saber-toothed tigers. And I can see why worry continues. There are real concerns, so real that they can be overwhelming and exhausting. I'm glad Luna is concerned about oil spills, excessive incarceration, homelessness, and disappearing glaciers, but only if it helps her think about how to help the world. I don't want her worries to keep her up all night. Our brains take time to figure out what kind of worrying is necessary for our safety, what kind might spur us to new inventions or righteous action, and what kind of worrying can make us sick.

Bobbie McFerrin debuted his hit song "Don't Worry, Be Happy" at my high school graduation. I jumped off the stage and danced with the rest of my class, but even then I had the sense that it was too simplistic a prescription. I don't think worrying is something inherently wrong that needs fixing. There is a lot to worry about. It's just that we could learn to worry more effectively.

"I don't think it's a disease, exactly," I told Luna. "We all worry, some more than others. The trick is to figure out when a worry is just bullying us and when it's something real."

"Does that mean you think it's kind of a disease?" Luna asked. Then, her voice quavering, she whispered, "Can it kill you? Is worrying a disease you can die from?"

"You absolutely cannot die from worrying," I say firmly, happy to be sure about something. I tell her worrying evolved to keep her safe and the only thing that worrying can do is get in the way of her enjoying herself and sleeping well.

Of course I would like Luna to worry less, and to "be happy" more. If there were a magic pill with no side effects that would make her lose all her unnecessary worries, I'd want her to have it, as long as it didn't erase her growing ability to see the world clearly, in all its inequality and uncertainty, all its unbearable ugliness and all its unbearable beauty.

When Luna was worried, I used to remind her to breathe slowly and deeply. Whenever a Buddhist teacher talked about breathing, it sounded so logical, so easy. Breathing, what a good idea! But it didn't work at all. Whenever I suggested mindful breathing, Luna would begin hyperventilating, taking loud shallow breaths and forcing the air out. Breathe into your belly, I'd suggest. "I *am!*" she'd wail, starting to cry. Neither Luna nor I were very good at breathing in our bellies. "Put your hand on your belly," I'd suggest. "That way you can feel your breath going in and out." "I *am!*" she'd say. "Then just BREATHE," I'd say, almost shouting. Soon, one or both of us would be laughing or crying.

Now, when Luna is upset I just try the breathing on my own. After a few deep breaths, I just ask Luna if she wants to breathe with me. Sometimes, she says yes. One hand on the belly, one on the heart, we see if we can move our hands with our breath. We don't correct each other or force each other to do it a special way. We just breathe together and, all the questions still there and unanswered, she falls asleep.

16. Crossing the Bridge

OFTEN MY KIDS' WORRIES take the form of "What if" questions. And while I can sometimes answer them directly and try and ease their fears, the answer I most often give is "We'll cross that bridge when we come to it." They want to know what that means and, in order to explain it, I tell them about the bridge on the commune.

Down the dirt path and across the junkyard from the main house where we all lived together, there was a crooked swinging bridge made of old rope and worn wooden slats, some missing. Beneath the bridge was a rocky creek that flowed from a trickle in the summer to a fast-moving and ice-cold rush in early spring. The bridge was maybe twelve feet above the creek and you wouldn't die if you fell through the slats, but you would probably break something.

I used to run across that bridge naked at full speed, loving the sound of the clickety clack of the slats as I stepped from one to the other, sometimes touching the rough and fraying rope for balance if I started to lean too far to one side or the other. We kids dared each other to run across it and gladly accepted the challenge because it was far scarier to cross slowly, the slats swaying to and fro with our weight and our fingers clutching tight to the thin and fraying rope.

That bridge is long gone, replaced by a sturdier wood one. But I still think of it when I'm worrying about something in the future. I can only cross that bridge when I come to it and not before. This doesn't mean that I don't first check the strength of the bridge or the fierceness of the water below. It doesn't mean that I forget where I'm going. My goals and intentions remain, but when I get to the bridge, I still look first. I don't assume how I will cross or focus on worrying about what will happen if the slat breaks. I don't want to be on my phone while I'm crossing, texting my friend: "Crossing bridge now! There in 5." I want to give my full attention to crossing the bridge. I can think about what happens on the other side when, and if, I get there.

The memory of this bridge has helped me learn to love a Buddhist practice that is also one of the most challenging. Most of my meetings with Thich Nhat Hanh had a pattern. After we drank our tea and talked about books, we would go for a walk, Thay and his attendant in front, the other monks and nuns and the rest of us walking behind. But this was not a normal walk. This was walking meditation and it went at such an excruciatingly slow pace that I rarely could go even a few feet without finding myself up ahead where Thay was, and then, embarrassed, dropping behind. I couldn't seem to make my feet go slow enough. I had thought sitting meditation was agonizing in the beginning, but I hadn't yet encountered walking meditation. Compared to walking meditation, sitting meditation was easy. If I was restless and rushing around inside my head while sitting still, no one was the wiser. In walking meditation, my restlessness would be visible. I had to focus completely on uniting body and mind just to be able to walk that slowly. There was no cheating.

Walking meditation is walking just for the awareness and joy of walking, without focusing on a destination. It's a good antidote to anxiety, because it reminds me that the next step is all I can take, and anything might happen after that. This is different from hiking or strolling, where you may not have a particular destination in mind, but you're still chatting with a friend or thinking about something other than what is right in front of you. Walking meditation is done by putting one foot in front of the other, paying attention to the shift in weight, lift, and touch of each step. This is all supposed to be done in rhythm with the breath and with joy and ease, without effort. Breathing in, I lift my foot. Breathing out, I put it down. Or breathing in, I take a step. Breathing out, I take another step. Some people practice matching the steps to the breaths exactly, others don't, but the focus is always on the relationship between the two.

Although I enjoyed the beauty of our walks, it took real effort to walk slowly enough, even considering the beauty of the monastery. Then in 2011, Thich Nhat Hanh was invited to give a talk at the Google headquarters in Mountain View, California. Over a hundred people put down their computers for an hour and practiced mindful breathing, and then we went outside to walk. It was fall, and already dark outside. The air had lost all memory of the sun. I was in a place that otherwise I would never be, a place where I had no associations or responsibilities. Despite the nap chairs, copious food stations, and glass walls and walkways in every building, the Google headquarters was cold. There were no public bookshelves, no library where one could curl up and read an actual printed book. I was aware of feeling fastidious with my already-old-fashioned ideas of what makes a place cozy.

We left the glass buildings for the concrete paths of the manicured grounds. Together, slowly, we walked past statues, abstract sculptures, and fountains. Maybe it was because I was away from any familiar place, or maybe it was just the right time, but I walked without effort. The walking and the breathing were my comfort, my home, and my sense of the familiar amidst the cold. We walked to walk and I didn't wonder where we were going or when it would end. After fifteen or so minutes of walking, Thay found a flat place by a concrete fountain and sat down. We all sat down with him. I huddled with a few nuns for warmth, our bodies sending the heat through the layers of robes, jackets, and scarves. Over a hundred of us sat there in silence, breathing, listening to the sounds of the fountain, our shared concentration like a humming virtual point of light reaching out into the cool night air.

The next summer, my family headed to the mountains for a month of no phone or electricity. One day, toward the end of our time there, I brought my camera to the river. As we walked home on the road, I scrolled through the pictures, irritated by the sounds of the river, the occasional car, and my kids chattering to each other. I was surprised by my irritation until I noticed that it was the first time in weeks that I'd tried to do two completely disconnected things that both required my attention. I'd gotten into the habit of just walking, and doing anything else at the same time felt like an intrusion.

I multi-task all day when I'm in the city and if I'm irritated by it, it's so familiar, I don't even notice. I don't remember being trained in how to do a hundred things at once, but on that walk up from the river I saw that multi-tasking wasn't a free way to get a lot of things done. Multi-tasking doesn't lessen my anxiety; it increases it. If, while crossing the bridge, I am focused on what's going to happen on the other side, I miss seeing the red bird that briefly rests on the rope. I miss noticing the beauty of the aged wood, or the idea for a story or a painting when I notice the way the missing slat makes a window down on to the river. Only when I do one thing at a time, shifting my attention and weight, breathing, taking one step and then another, do I become open to whatever is in front of me. Only then do all the possibilities of the moment emerge.

17. Monks in the Ocean

IT WAS MY ANNUAL MEETING WITH THAY to talk about creating new titles for the coming year. We were outside his hut at Deer Park Monastery in Escondido and he was lying in his hammock. I was sitting on a pillow on the floor. We drank tea. After a little while, he said, "I think we should publish a book on the environment. I've been talking a lot about the Earth. I think, this would be a very pleasurable book to work on."

I agreed.

"Perhaps," he said, "it will be so enjoyable that you will publish it in just ten days." I told him I thought it would take longer. We had to transcribe the talks. I had to edit it. He had to read it. It would take a few weeks to finish it and design it and send it to the printer and then the printer would need a few weeks to get it back to us. Okay, he said, maybe a little more time. There were a few more minutes of silence. "But still," Thay finally said, "make sure to do it joyfully."

Then it was time to go to the beach. Thay's attendant packed the travel hammock. Lunch was made. I jumped in the car with a few nuns. We didn't know exactly where we were going. The nun in the back seat was a backseat driver, offering many suggestions. The nun who was driving smiled gently and continued driving just as she had been. I vowed to copy that same smile the next time I was at the wheel and Jason was gasping, groaning, and gripping the handle of the passenger door.

When we got to the beach, I realized I hadn't brought a swimsuit. Did the monks and nuns have brown swimsuits to match their brown robes? Did they travel with brown wetsuits that covered their whole bodies? I figured we would all just sit there and breathe mindfully and look at the ocean. We had a delicious vegetarian picnic. Then Thay's attendant set up his hammock between two skinny palm trees and soon Thay was fast asleep. I stared out at the Pacific Ocean. It was a warm, calm day, with a slight breeze that kept the hammock swaying. The Southern California coast is flatter than it is up north. Miles and miles of nothing but white sand and dune buggies and surfers. Way out in the ocean, I saw what looked like a seal on a boogie board. There were a few of them, their brown skin wrapped in what looked like folds around their bodies as they held tight to the boards. I looked closer. It was the monks, still in their robes, soaking wet and far out in the ocean.

Inspired, I walked to the water's edge. Sister Chan Khong, one of the first nuns to be ordained in Thay's tradition, joined me. The water was cold, but not freezing. It swirled around our legs, bathing us, as if to say, don't be afraid to get wet. More monks and nuns went in. Others were happy just to watch. There were no requirements, just the openness to enjoy the experience in whatever way you wanted. When the monks climbed out of the sea, Thay awoke, we all gathered our belongings, and salty and sandy, returned to our cars. The nun in the backseat with me closed her eyes and rested, too tired from her time in the ocean to talk.

About nine months later, with as much joy as I could muster, we published Thay's book about the environment.

18. Stranded on the Number 9

WHEN I COMMIT to not waiting and not holding back, I open myself up to feelings of pure joy. They creep up on me and remind me to let go when, despite loving the thrill of attack and paddle, I get scared and hold back. It's not just fear of pain that can hold me back; I'm afraid that I will experience joy and then it will be gone.

I met Jason twenty years ago on a bus in Seattle. I was twenty-two. I took the bus every morning to work as a program coordinator at a public elementary school. The long bumpy bus ride wound through Seattle's still mostly segregated neighborhoods—from the predominantly European-American neighborhood of Ravenna, with its old stone houses, through the Vietnamese and Ethiopian neighborhoods of the Central District, to the historic African American neighborhood of Rainier Valley.

I'm too much of a people-watcher to be able to read on the bus, so the long ride inspired me to take up crocheting. My specialty was hats. This was a very practical niche, given the constantly cold and gray Seattle weather. Unfortunately, I was a very impatient crocheter. I'd hurry to finish each one in just a couple of rides and my hats always turned into doll hats, too small for anyone but the tiniest baby. I had no dolls or small babies to give them to, so they'd end up stuffed in a drawer in the back of my closet.

I always sat toward the back of the bus and generally, while crocheting, I stared at the neck of a man who sat near the front. He always wore a trucker's hat, one that actually fit his large head, and a Carhartt jacket, the kind made out of that flame-resistant heavy duty cotton duck that keeps its shape even when you take it off. There was a one-inch strip of neck visible where his jacket collar ended and his hat began, and it was at this band of creamy skin that I would stare as I crocheted.

One day, about halfway to my stop, the bus sputtered, slowed, and pulled to the side. I looked up from my latest small purple half-crocheted hat. There were a few small technical issues, the bus driver announced, but we should be moving shortly. Time passed. People started milling around and talking to each other. A few people got off the bus. I found myself standing next to the guy in the Carhartt jacket. "You going to wait?" he asked.

"Yeah," I said, "I work at a school down in the Rainier Valley. What about you?"

"I don't work far," he said, "I'm going to walk." He smiled and headed out the door. Out the window, I saw the top of his hat and jacket collar saunter by, the thin band of neck obscured by the angle of my high view.

The next week was spring break. My mom came to visit and I took some time off work. When I got back on the bus a week later, the guy with the jacket wasn't there. He wasn't there the next day either, or the next. Eventually, I switched my attention to another regular, an old woman who usually sat in the very first seat. Though I missed looking at the back of my old friend's neck as I crocheted, the elegance of her stiff and starched gray curls was some consolation.

About a month after I stopped seeing the man on the bus, I went for coffee in the café on the corner. There was a line and so I picked up the local free paper, *The Stranger*, while I waited. In the back of the paper, in the section called I Saw You, was this ad:

Stranded on the Number 9 to Rainier Valley
You have dark hair, a green hat, and work
at an elementary school.
I work for an artist. We talked. Let's talk again.
Box #5496

It was the jacket man. In this era before cell phones, I had to wait until I got home to call him. He called back the next night and we arranged to meet at a café whose crème brulee I still remember almost twenty years later. I wasn't sure at first if it was him. I'd looked at the back of his neck so often, I hadn't really noticed his face. And he'd gotten a haircut. He seemed startled by my arrival and we stumbled through small talk, slowly beginning to enjoy each other only as the night came to an end.

Too bad nothing will come of it, I thought when we parted. He seemed like a really nice guy. He called again, though, and we met on a hill in an old toxic gas works that had been converted into a park. We spent most of the time together reassuring each other that neither of us was looking for a serious relationship. We continued reassuring each other of this for the next ten years, as we moved from Seattle to Manhattan to Brooklyn, until we finally sat down at another industrial park, this one overlooking the East River, and, huddled together on a spray-painted piece of steel, admitted we were starting to get serious.

∞

Like many children of divorced parents, I have always been determined to avoid divorce—and marriage is the first step to divorce. Since marriage often requires planning and paperwork, I was pretty sure I could avoid the whole thing as long as I never went to Las Vegas.

But since the whole point of avoiding divorce is to avoid the hurt, not just the paperwork, this strategy required that I stayed less invested in any relationship than the other person. I never called first. I never let myself ask to see someone again. I always had a backup plan. And I took things very, very slowly.

Jason and I were involved for seven years, in two cities, before we ever lived together. When we finally did move into the same house, it was a big, communal loft in Brooklyn with four other people. We were together eleven years before we lived together as a couple, with no one else, and since I was eight months pregnant at that point, it was more like the three of us. Even then, we lived in a duplex with my close friend, her husband, and their baby right downstairs.

Part of the reason for the crowd is just my communal up-bringing. I like having people around. There is always someone up for a late-night talk, or to watch the baby, or to help cook. My favorite way to fall asleep is still in the middle of the party, curled up on the couch with voices all around me. But part of it was an instinctive sense that it's best not to rely on one person, in case he decides to go out for cigarettes one day and never comes back. The more people around, the better the chance of someone to help, or someone to talk to. Thay recommends that every person have a *sangha*, a community safety net. The more people in my safety net, the fewer holes.

Despite my best efforts, though, I have found myself com-pletely and totally attached. Two years ago, Jason, who has never needed to go to a doctor or even a dentist in all the time I've known him, ended up in the emergency room with septic appen-dicitis. Due to a doctor's error, his operation was delayed and by the time his ruptured appendix was removed, he was quite sick. He was in the hospital for a week, unable to eat and barely able to walk. Seeing him push himself slowly around the hospital floor, the back flap of his gown barely closed, I was done holding back. I was going to love him proudly, openly, and without reserve for whatever limited time we have together.

I had hoped to remain unattached enough so that I wouldn't be too hurt if and when the other person left. But if Buddhism has taught me anything, it is that no matter what, the other person always leaves. He may walk out for cigarettes and never come back or he may leave slowly, after months in a hospital bed. Impermanence means we all leave.

After two children, a house, and twenty years, Jason and I have yet to get married. Old superstitions die hard. But if we do wed, we will use this wedding blessing by the Buddhist teacher Eric Kolvig:

> As surely as this wedding joins you, death or estrange-
> ment will part you. I hope that you will never take
> for granted what can never be taken for granted. If
> you know in your hearts every day that you will lose
> each other, then you can cut away attachment with
> the fierce courage of a fox that chews off its own leg
> to free itself from the trap. If you know for certain
> this approaching loss, perhaps every day you can thank
> each other for the invaluable gift of that day together.
> Perhaps this knowing will help you live gratefully and
> urgently together in the present moment.[*]

For most of the years Jason and I have been together, whenever we fought, I would plan my exit. I comforted myself by thinking of what friend's house or hotel I could run off to, what five things I would bring, and how I would never look back. Even sharing children and a home did not cure me of my illusion that I could

[*]Eric Kolvig, "A Wedding Blessing," http://erickolvig.com/?p=17.

disentangle myself without too many scars. But his illness, and the small aches and pains of my own aging, have convinced me of something that all of Thay's words could not. I can't escape our connection and I can't escape the pain of our separation, however and whenever it comes. He can still be horribly, obstinately wrong. So can I. But I hold my anger differently. It no longer makes me think I have to move immediately into action. In the morning after a fight, I know that if I am still there and he is still there lying next to me, it's not because I have compromised too much or given in. It's because we are lucky enough to have one more day

19. Raise Your Hand If You're Going to Die

I FIRST BECAME AWARE of the finality of death in an outhouse when I was six years old. We were living on the commune and I'd started up the hill to the screened-in outhouse with its couple of wooden benches and a shorter children's bench. It was set up to accommodate six bottoms at the same time, and sometimes it did. The trick to having some privacy was to carefully observe the grown-ups' routine and then make a run for it during the off moments. If I stood at the apple tree behind the main house and craned my neck, I could double-check the occupancy. To be absolutely sure of having the space to myself, I would sing on the way up, in the hopes that if anyone was in there they would call out a hello and I could change direction.

On this day, after confirming that the outhouse was empty, I went inside. I was confident enough of my solitude that I picked up one of the *National Geographic* magazines lying around. The cover story was about the recent discoveries of ancient Egyptian civilization. This was during the famous Treasures of Tutankhamen tour and the era of Steve Martin's song, "King Tut," which was so popular it even reached our electricity-free mountain commune. I studied the illustrations of women and children walking together, people cooking, a market, a procession. With their curly dark hair, strong noses, and olive skin, some of these people looked like they could be related to me. A whole civilization had lived and thrived, doing all the things people do, with no idea they would one day completely disappear.

The idea that I could die and be gone completely, that there would be no trace I had ever lived, was terrifying. I took short shallow breaths, willing myself to get off the toilet and out of the outhouse, but I was unable to move. For the first time I understood that people don't just die—they completely disappear. I understood the inevitability of death and I wanted no part of it.

From that point on, I thought about death a lot. If I was swimming in a fast river or crossing the old hanging bridge, I would picture my demise as if watching it on a screen. Even lying in bed at night, safe and warm, I imagined my skin cold by morning. It wasn't an early death that concerned me, it was death, period. I could not escape the inevitable erasure of my existence. Many times I awoke in the middle of the night in a panic, knowing there was nothing I could do about the fact that I would one day die.

I would like to say this was a phase. The Hungarian psychologist Maria Nagy found that most children between the ages of five and nine begin to understand that death is final and that the dead stay dead. Before that, kids tend to think the dead are very sleepy and might or might not wake up. But even though older children understand that death is final, Nagy found that many kids at that age still think death is something that happens to other people—people who are sick or old, people who jumped off high rocks or went outside in the rain without a jacket. It is only after children have reached the age of nine or ten, Nagy found, that they comprehend what she calls Stage 3, the personal nature of death. Everybody dies, whether they are nice or mean, ant or elephant, stranger or parent.

But I don't think many of us fully make it to Stage 3. We know, on some level, that death doesn't just happen to other people, but most of us still think that our continued life, despite possible accidents and the deaths of others, must be in some part due to our luck, karma, cleverness, good spirits, or diligence in taking our vitamins.

My children have never seen a dead person up close. In the few funerals they have been to, the dead person is represented by images of their life—photos and personal effects—as if it was a party in their honor and they'd just stepped out. Their lack of familiarity with death is both a matter of our particular family's way of doing things and also part of the larger American cultural commitment to the illusion of the innocence of childhood.

Death stays mostly hidden in U.S. society. People don't usually die at home. Funerals rarely wind through the streets, as they used to in New Orleans and still do in many parts of the world, and cremations tend to be done in sterile, closed-off facilities, instead of all-night outdoor bonfires.

This denial has been helpful in keeping my fear of death at bay. I can just push it away and get on with my life, as long as no one brings it up. But the way my children deal with fear is to talk about it. They are determined to make discussions about death part of daily life. The other morning Plum was putting on her pink sneakers for school. She looked up cheerfully from tying her laces and, apropos of nothing, said, "Raise your hand if you don't want to die."

We all raised our hands.

My kids see dead things all around them every day. These are little creatures mostly, dead spiders or dehydrated moths, fossils, or the stuffed creatures in the natural history museum. At the beach, we find dried-out crabs and an occasional fish skeleton. When we're driving, they see the bloodied remains of raccoons and possums and other critters who had unlucky crossings.

They haven't yet seen a dead human being, though they talk about the grown-ups they know who have died. Last summer, on the curvy pass just down the road from the treehouse where we live during the summers, a woman that we knew drove too fast and too drunk at night and went over the cliff, dying instantly. She was a mother of two girls, a two-year-old and a five-year-old. We were down the road when it happened, and saw the car, over the edge, on our morning walk. She was not the first person we knew to die on that road, but it was the first time I saw a crumpled car and knew that somebody had just been inside.

When they found out what had happened, Plum said, "Aw, that's sad," and was done. Luna wanted to know how fast the woman was going, why she didn't stop, and how much alcohol is too much for driving. She wanted to know about the dad, and if he was nice and if he was going to take good care of the kids.

Back in the city, Luna started waking up at 2:30 in the morning, panicked after a recurring dream in which I died and she was left all alone. She's old enough to know it was a dream, but also old enough to know that sometimes parents do die when their children are little.

Plum is just down on death in general. She cries when she sees a picture of a heron eating a shrimp. On the river, she attacked a young friend of ours who drowned a butterfly in the hopes of using it as a fishing lure. When we pulled her off of him, our eight-year-old friend Emma who lives on the river year-round, said, slightly astonished by Plum's fury, "But Plum, everything dies."

"I know!" Plum wailed. "And I don't like it."

Plum wants to know why, when you die, "you don't grow up again." When I tell her you get to grow as part of the earth, part of the compost or the flowers, she wants to know how I know this. She wants to know if you get to pick what you become next.

We talk about probability, chances, imagination, reality, and how we have to make so many of our decisions based on what will likely happen as opposed to what may be a tiny chance of happening. And we talk about death, whenever we see it.

My mother is a midwife and my kids are used to birth. They've seen babies get born. They've touched a placenta or two. They understand where a cervix is. They've seen photos and videos of births and have heard so many birth stories that, except for occasional games of playing midwife and baby, they tune them out. But even if they hadn't, they'd still be in a culture where birth is celebrated and acknowledged all around them. They see the birth announcements, come to the baby showers, and join the endless conversations about baby names. And yet every birth is also the beginning of a death.

Perhaps if death was as acknowledged and visible as birth, awareness and acceptance of it would become more commonplace. With more public mourning, more obvious and communal ritual, my kids and I could possibly get more used to the intense certainty of people dying. It wouldn't be our private fear, our own daily negotiation. "Raise your hand if you're going to die," Plum could say. And we'd all calmly raise our hands.

20. Touching Dead People

EVERY *DIA DE LOS MUERTOS,* the Mexican holiday of honoring the dead, our family makes a small altar to the loved ones who have died in our family and community. Usually, it is just a few pictures, a candle, maybe a marigold or a cookie, and a hard-worked drawing of a dancing skeleton that Luna and Plum made. They also write notes to their great-grandmother, whom they called GGMa, who died a few years ago. *Hi GGMa. I ♥ U. Love, Plum.*

Afterwards, Luna and Plum usually spend a little time talking about what happens when you die. Luna has decided that you have two choices when you die: to be in a coffin, which means to become compost with the worms, or to become ashes. We haven't yet discussed sky or sea burial and other less familiar options. She says she's personally leaning toward being ashes. She also accepts my vague explanation that when you die your cells become part of "everything that exists"—the air, the soil, the water, the flowers, and the earth.

Of course, Luna has passed all this vast knowledge of death on to Plum. "I wish you would live to a hundred, Plum, but you're probably only going to live until ninety-two. That's more likely. But don't worry; you're still little. You're not even close to ninety-two."

Plum thinks about the future Luna has laid out before her. "If you're old," she asks "and you get sick, then you die? Is that the only way?"

"You become part of the dirt," Luna says wisely. "So when you're digging in the dirt and playing, you're touching dead people. There are probably dead people on your hands right now."

"Oh," Plum says, examining her fingernails.

At some point after this conversation, Plum got really scared. She'd recently stopped sucking her thumb, in order not to mess up her nail polish, and now the floodgates of worry were open each night. We made time to talk about death and other worries in the light of day, setting aside time after waffles on Sunday morning or on the couch in the afternoon, so that she wouldn't associate worrying and nighttime, but to no avail. She still worked herself up every evening before bed.

It came down to this: She didn't want to die. She didn't want Ausencio, who runs our favorite taco truck on Ashby Avenue, to die. She didn't want doctors to die, because then who would help her when she's sick? And she didn't want really old people to die either. She didn't want to become "part of everything that exists" because she was already part of it and she didn't want to become a tree or a flower because people cut down trees and they pick flowers.

During the day, Plum and I spend some time on the Buddhist allegory of the relationship of the wave to the ocean. This is one of Thay's favorite metaphors. It makes sense to me, and seems easy enough to translate to Plum. We talk about how the wave rises and falls, and how it's not separate from the continuous ocean. This life is like the wave, I tell her. We came from the water and we will continue to be the water after our life rises and falls.

"Yes," she says, "but will I be able to see when I'm dead?"

I explain how when you're dead, you don't have to worry, because nothing can hurt you, and Luna says, "Yeah, Plum, some people even kill themselves when they could be alive because they want to be dead." Plum laughs, surprised.

I go for a platitude: "No matter what, I'll always be with you and you'll always be safe, even when you die." Plum, however, wants to get specific. "Does that mean you'll lie on the hard ground next to me? We'll be really still and hold hands and then we'll both die?"

No, I tell her sadly, it doesn't mean that.

"What if a bulldozer falls on our house and squishes my bed while you're in the other room?" "What if a tornado comes and I can't get to the basement?" "What if we get really tiny all of a sudden and you can't see us?"

She has more questions than I can answer. How does the body actually die? Can you die from "eating alcohol"? Can you die from smoking? Can you die when you're a kid? From being sick?

I remind her that we are like the waves, rising and falling, and suggest we shelve the discussion until the morning in favor of falling off to sleep and dreaming of clouds or flowers or choco-late. But no matter what I say or how early we go to bed, she has to go through what the psychologist Elisabeth Kübler-Ross calls "the five stages of grief" each evening. She starts with denial ("If I have to die, then I don't want to be a person"), then anger ("I wish babies died first!"), bargaining ("Can I be 500 years old when I die?"), depression ("I hate death and I hate everything"), and sometimes, just out of exhaustion, acceptance ("If I have to die, then I want to be a flower snuggled around your flower, Mama"). I tell her that we can't know the details, we just know we're in it together. I stroke her head and sing about horses and flowers and rivers. Eventually this works and she falls asleep. In the morning, she wakes up cheerful, excited that her fancy nail polish is still intact.

21. The Five Remembrances

EACH MORNING, as we are getting ready for school, Plum says to me, "Tell me again why we have to die." This is my own reminder to stay awake. Death is a part of life, unwilling to be ignored.

When I get to work I have another reminder. The Five Remembrances, part of a Buddhist sutra called the Upajjhatthana Sutta, are pinned above my desk. The Five Remembrances remind me that everything changes, every single thing. The first three remembrances remind me that it's not my inherent specialness, self-discipline, or intelligence that gives me good health and life. The fourth remembrance reminds me to appreciate the loved ones around me and the fifth reminds me of my responsibility to my loved ones and to the world. The first time I read them, I hated them.

1. *I am of the nature to grow old. There is no way to escape growing old.*

"Shut up," I said. "That's a long way off. There's no point in thinking about it now."

2. *I am of the nature to have ill health. There is no way to escape ill health.*

I'm unusually healthy, I reminded myself. I rarely even have a cold. I plan to be healthy until I'm hit by a car and die, so this one really doesn't apply to me.

3. I am of the nature to die. There is no way to escape death.

This one I'll admit to. But it won't happen for a long, long, long, long time. Can we talk about something else?

4. All that is dear to me and everyone I love are of the nature to change. There is no way to escape being separated from them.

"Everyone dies," Luna told Plum the other night.

"I KNOW," says Plum. People are always telling her things she already knows. "Even Dexter is going to die." Dexter is her friend Serena's brother. We met him once at the local taqueria. He is five.

"Dexter won't die until he's probably ninety-four," Luna says. Somehow, she knows everything. "Serena will probably live until she's ninety-five or ninety-six."

"I think ninety-six," says Plum. "Or ninety-eight," she adds.

"Probably not ninety-eight," says Luna.

They're both quiet for a moment, contemplating Serena's demise.

"Who is going to die first, Luna?" Plum asks. "Me or you?"

I have listened to this whole conversation without saying a word. Now, though, I bite my lip, hard.

"I don't know exactly when we are going to die," Luna finally admits. "But I promise I'll stay with you till it happens."

5. My actions are my only true belongings. I cannot escape the conse-quences of my actions. My actions are the ground upon which I stand.

Buddhism defines karma as the triple action of our words, thoughts, and physical actions and the fruits of these actions that continue into the world long after we are gone. It's the reward for struggling through all the nonattachment and for all the diligence of paying attention. I don't know if the compost that I will one day become will sprout a flower next to Plum's flower, but I do believe that my thoughts, words, and actions continue to have an impact after I'm gone. Once they're out in the world, they can't be taken back. Our well-being, this reminds us, depends on us being fully engaged with the world. Our involvement is not just a matter of having a hobby or doing what is morally right. Our involvement with others is the ground upon which we stand.

Thay says that the greatest relief you can get from Buddhist practice is to go beyond the notion of birth and death, of thinking you are going to die, and of believing that your life only lasts these eighty or a hundred years. What we say, what we do, and what we think matters not just for our lifetime but for the world after we're gone. For me, this isn't as good as getting to stay alive forever, but it's better than the alternative.

22. The Real Meaning of Karma

I AM SITTING in a meeting with Thich Nhat Hanh. Though he is eighty-six, he looks the same as when I met him ten years ago. Our meeting is unhurried and quiet, as our meetings tend to be. There is a lot of time to stop and drink tea in between comments. At some point in the meeting, the light from the window is shining in someone's eyes. A young monk starts to get up to close the curtain, but Thay jumps up and beats him to it. Then he sits down and smiles. "See," he says, "I'm still young."

Thay doesn't seem to mind aging. I feel younger and younger each day, he says. Truly. I don't feel that the disintegration of this body means my end because I am able to see 'me' alive in other forms all around me. I have invested myself in so many people who are now the continuation of me, just as I am the continuation of those before me. So I don't consider this body to be me."

I, however, still consider my body to be a big part of "me," at least for now, but I find very comforting the idea that our investment in others is our continuation after we die. It is the flip side to the stark truth that everything, including our bodies, is changing, ending, impermanent. Our continuation is our karma.

I used to think of karma as instant retribution and conse-
quences. I thought it was the idea that if you did something bad,
bad things would happen to you; if you did something nice, you'd
get nice things. But I wasn't seeing much instant karma. I remember a particularly hard year when I went to a new elementary
school. A few kids would call me names or try to trip me. One
kid came up to me, slapped me and then skipped merrily away.
No piano fell from the sky and squashed these kids. Although I
watched closely, for the whole rest of the school year none of the
mean kids developed boils or warts. I was not consoled by my
mother's suggestion that they were probably unhappier than I
was inside or had some hidden challenge. I was plenty unhappy
on the inside. And if my third-grade tormenter ever did develop
an affliction, it would be so far in the future that he wouldn't realize it was because he'd been mean to me and it wouldn't make
him nicer. I decided karma took too long. It didn't work. I was
going to have to take karma into my own hands.

I was at least partly right about karma; we do need to take it
into our own hands. It's not a physical thing we get back; rather
it's what remains from our being in the world after everything
else leaves. Karma literally means "action." Nothing stays the
same. Everything disintegrates and changes. But our thoughts,
speech, and physical actions remain and their influence remains.

Thay puts it like this: A pine tree doesn't have to do anything but be a pine tree in order to contribute to its environment.
But unlike that pine tree, we have the ability to think, to speak,
and to act. If the pine tree could move and act, we'd say, "Come

on pine tree—get out there and pick up that soda can someone threw on the ground. While you're at it, can you move over a little bit so you're not blocking the light for that other little tree?" Of course, then it wouldn't be a pine tree. It's our humanity that gives us the ability to think, speak, and act.

Whatever I produce in terms of thought, speech, and action is my continuation, my karma. So while karma can't drop a piano on a schoolyard bully, knowing that my karma is what I will leave behind when my body is gone helps push me to speak up for myself and others and, some days, makes the prospect of aging and dying seem less final.

Thay says that after the dissolution of this body, you continue in other forms. It's like the cloud in the sky. After the cloud disappears from the sky, it manifests in the rain, the snow, the hail, and the water for my tea. It is impossible for your cloud to die, to pass from being into nonbeing. It's impossible for you to die. You can't pass from being into nonbeing. With your karma, you continue always.

This reminds me that the little and big things I do in the world reverberate. The words I help teenagers and grown authors put down on the page will contiunue long after the writer is gone. The shouts of the protests in the streets will change laws long after the street has been swept of protesters. I teach my kids to take care of the world as I take care of them, so that the effects of our caring will continue long after we are gone.

23. How to Raise Happy Grown-ups

WHEN I WAS GROWING UP, my mother used to say that the only thing she wanted for me was for me "to be happy." This was infuriating because it was so blatantly false. It's not that she didn't want me to be happy; it's just that she had some very specific and immutable ideas about what could and should constitute this happiness. Being good at gymnastics, playing the piano, singing, and getting a lot of sleep all seemed to figure large in her sense of happiness—but not, unfortunately, in mine. I rarely wanted to sleep. I was unexceptional at gymnastics and worse on the piano. I sang off-key. The two things I was really good at, reading and arguing, didn't seem to figure in her plan.

Like her mother, Luna excels at reading and arguing, but she has no interest in the one thing I was sure was necessary to her happiness: milking goats. During my childhood on the commune, milking goats was one of my greatest pleasures, and so a couple years ago I went to great lengths to find some goats for my city-born kids to milk. At Slide Ranch, less than two hours away, I found Fiona, a white Alpine goat. She was even-tempered, not too large, and smelled wonderful. Luna refused to have anything to do with her. I pleaded, cajoled, begged, and briefly considered forcing her. Then I gave up. All the restless parents with their thrilled-to-be-goat-milking children were about to push us out of the way anyhow.

I have a whole set of ideas in my head, many of them half-conscious, about the requisite ingredients for happiness. Before I became a parent, I'd resolved not to push them onto my yet un-born children. Of course, now that they're here, it's harder. But one of the good things about teaching my kids about karma and their continuation is that it reminds me that happiness, in and of itself, is not the point.

Recently, a popular article warned us that "our obsession with our kids' happiness may be dooming them to unhappy adulthoods."* Is there really evidence that parents who are try-ing "too hard" to make their children happy are actually making their children unhappy? I'm all for a little more detachment and a lot less helicoptering in the general parenting world, but I don't think those parents who are velcroed to their kids are keeping those kids from being happy. The culprit is a little larger than that: the whole notion that if we just parent them right, our kids will grow into happy adults despite being surrounded by ineq-uity, injustice, exploitation, and climate disintegration.

When Luna was born, attachment parenting was all the rage. As I'd managed to avoid every parenting book and article on the planet, as well as many other actual parents, I'd never heard of it. I went back to work at six weeks, bringing Luna with me. Most of the time I practiced exhaustion parenting, which consisted of

*Lori Gottlieb, "How to Land Your Kid in Therapy," *The Atlantic*, July/August 2011, www.theatlantic.com/magazine/archive/2011/07/how-to-land-your-kid-in-therapy/8555/.

doing whatever was easiest and was often indistinguishable from doing the only thing that seemed possible. Around me, everyone seemed to have found a parenting religion. Parents were practicing "evacuation communication" (involving no diapers and lots of changes of clothes), or carrying their baby everywhere, so the baby's feet didn't touch the ground. Other parents we knew were having their six-month-old baby "cry it out" for up to thirty minutes at a time or following Magda Gerber's Resources for Infant Educators philosophy of body awareness and adamantly arguing against "tummy time" or any forced movement of a child's body. By the time Plum was born, it was all about teaching your small child resilience and sign language, letting life knock her around and then reminding her that all that hurt and anger were just "feelings," and making sure she didn't eat too much soy or carbohydrates.

My kids are surrounded by kids who were raised all these ways. They are all quite different from each other, of course, but there's no way I could pick, by a few-hour observation, which one was raised by which philosophy. With the exception of those whose parents are notably obsequious or oblivious, these kids are coming fully into themselves, with distinct quirks and comforts. The one who slept in his parents' bed until he was five and nursed until he was four is neither more confident or more tentative than the one whose parent stopped breastfeeding at nine months and strictly complied with the "cry it out" method at six months.

This is perhaps what psychoanalyst Donald Winnicott called the "good enough" parenting model. Basically, as long as you were clearly loved and allowed to develop without too much interference, even if your parents messed up a lot and were either over- or underprotective, you're all right. Of course, it's too early to know how Luna and her peers will turn out and how closely we'll be able to trace their neuroses to our early parenting decisions, but my guess is the uncomfortable truth that parents only have so much influence.

I believe in the "happy enough" model. I'd like my kids to grow up to feel focused and do work that is meaningful for them and for the world. I'd like them to feel like their lives are important and useful, and I'd love it if they experienced some sense of equanimity mixed with those precious moments of joy. But I don't want them to be blithely ignorant, happy adults.

Your parenting cannot guarantee that your kid will grow up to be a happy grownup. But if you're doing a good enough job, chances are it's not your parenting that is going to make your kid unhappy either. It's life. Even back in Siddhartha's time, before the onslaught of parenting books and hovering parents and life coaches, he came upon the world's (and every teenager's) first noble truth: Life is suffering. I don't think Siddhartha thought this because his mother was overprotective, or not fulfilled enough in her relationship with his father, or had gone back to work after he was born. I think kids instinctively know that if things aren't okay out there in the world—and they're not—they can't really feel safe and secure. If we want to raise the chances of our kids having happier lives, we need to focus on making the world a happier place.

Kids have an inherent sense that things should be fair and they can tell when we're working to make them more fair. They'll reflect either the sense of entitlement or the sense of fairness that their grownups model. In a way, it's a relief. Our individual choices get a break, but our conduct in the rest of the world gets more scrutiny. We are not responsible for our children's happiness, but we are responsible for that of the whole world.

PART III

Connected

24. Me, Myself, and Interbeing

THE SECOND NOBLE TRUTH is that our attachment to our views is the cause of our suffering. The most deeply ingrained wrong view, the one that most of us will need pried from our cold, dead hands, is our view that we are each individual, separate selves. According to the Buddha, all my unease about aging and dying, my clinging to life, apparently comes from my illusion that I have an individual unchanging separate self.

I know at some level that my self-ness is an illusion; in part because I can see it in my children and in all the people I know and love. I get that they are not just "my" children or my loved ones. They are cellularly connected to all that came before them, and to all the things—sun, air, food, warmth, love—that keep them alive. But even knowing this to be true, and even knowing that I, like them, am dependent on the elements all around me, I am a firm believer in the illusion of a separate self.

Although that illusion is the cause of my greatest fear and suffering, it also brings me my greatest joy and pleasure. I love being with my thoughts and my particularities. My own opinions and emotions and my creativity and dreams bring me so much pleasure that I would not trade my sense of a separate self for anything, even if it means I could get rid of my fear of death and the suffering that attachment brings me.

At the same time, aging and mindfulness have finally drilled it into me that on every level—cellular, physical, emotional, and spiritual—I cannot exist by myself, nor do I want to. As I write this, it is summer in the Siskiyou Mountains. I have escaped the chaos of guests and mess and am sitting alone in a small tree-house. I feel rather independent up here, even as I am completely reliant on all the people who made the parts of this computer I'm using; the geese whose feathers fill the down sleeping bag that keeps my feet warm; the sunshine, rain, and food that went into keeping those geese healthy and alive; the people whose work went into the creation, manufacturing, and distribution of the sweatshirt I'm wearing; and the trees whose logs made these walls. Then there are the hundreds of living orangisms that keep the forest healthy and the creek that runs alongside the treehouse flowing with clear, clean water.

Interbeing is the idea that we're not just all connected in some Facebook-type way, but that our very existence depends on each other and on all living things and that their existence depends on us. And though I'm not letting go of my separate self yet, interbeing is the Buddhist concept I find easiest to accept. Partly this is because I was brought up on a commune and saw early on that other people are not optional. Partly this is because I see it everyday in my children and keep it alive in the myriad characters daily coming in and out of our house that we call our community. Partly this is because interbeing is so visible. We can see that babies require grown-ups and that tomato plants require sunlight, rainfall, oxygen and compost. My kids have a clear understanding, though they don't always like it, that there can't be day without night or warmth without cold.

The logical consequence of this teaching is that mindful awareness is not just about making me feel less stressed. While I feel more relaxed and at ease, I'm also more aware of my connection and responsibility to all the other living beings. Social responsibility and active engagement becomes not just a hobby, but a requirement for being fully alive.

Being available for the present moment is much more pleasant when we realize that others are there, too. Buddhism calls these other people our sangha, our practice community. I call them my sanity. I need this quiet focused time. Most days, I have three separate times when I stop and breathe with other people (even though sometimes it's still torture for the first few moments). After preparing six breakfasts (including those for the family, one for the person inevitably staying in our guest room, one for the outside cat), four lunches, prepping a dinner, and getting all of us out the door, I arrive at work. We have our fifteen solid minutes of sitting before getting down to the rest of our business. In the evening, after the cooking and homework and running around, we invite the bell and sit in silence before we begin to eat and tell our stories. Then at night, during martial arts training, we all—over forty teenagers and adults of every size, shape, and color—sit together in silence before we begin practicing, punching and kicking each other.

Although I'm still prone to impatience and fidgeting, I emerge from these short moments of collective silence different from when I began. The rushing around, the overload, the insecurities and aspirations don't disappear, but they pause long enough for me to notice the individual faces, bright colors, and fresh air around me. The quality of this time together, the coming together in awareness, is so different from all the time I spend just passing others in space, each of us unavailable to the moment or to each other. Sitting together, the breath of our community unites us, and the power of our silence is magnified.

25. Many-Colored Cocoons

I FIRST EXPERIENCED SANGHA on the commune. Everyone came with different backgrounds and agendas, and there were a lot of arguments, as well as a lot of parties. Because we were living in the country, there were also many moments of beautiful silence. Grown-ups usually fell into two groups, the dreamers versus the doers, and us kids figured out pretty quickly who to go to for a good story and who to go to for something to eat. Most of the time, we roamed freely, knowing we'd be familiar with any grown-up we eventually came across.

After we moved to the city, I found that sense of community in political protest. This was the San Francisco Bay Area in the late seventies and early eighties. Nuclear weapons and nuclear energy were on everyone's minds and the groups that came together to protest were made up of a lot of the former commune people and those that, if they weren't from the commune, could easily have been. People were often argumentative, prone to long meetings that lasted into the night, willing to give me a snack if I was hungry or a sweatshirt if I was cold, and motivated, for the most part, by the attempt to create a more compassionate and safe world for future generations.

I got arrested for the first time when I was thirteen years old. The arms race was at its height. Every time I crossed the Bay Bridge, I imagined a bomb exploding and I'd think, "This is the last thought I'll ever have." My nightmares were full of red flames and melting steel. My stepsister and I had started a group for kids who were opposed to nuclear weapons and we had decided to join the massive protest that was trying to shut down Lawrence Livermore Laboratory, the local lab that designs nuclear weapons. Our group's thinking was morally clear: Nuclear weapons killed thousands of people indiscriminately, so there was no way to use them ethically or safely. I'd written many letters to various officials, newspapers, and politicians asking them to stop funding nuclear weapon development, with no response. It was worth it to try and stop nukes from being made.

We made armbands, choreographed songs and dances, and took a workshop on what to do if and when we were arrested. We had emergency numbers written on our arms in Sharpie, secret stashes of almonds, and warm jackets. All the kids and grownups spent the night in a nearby church. I awoke in the night, unused to the sounds of snoring and rustling around me. In the dim light, our many-colored sleeping bags huddled together on the cold floor looked like a mass of vulnerable cocoons.

We got up at three in the morning so we could be there to sit down in the road and block the entrance to the nuclear facility before the workers arrived. We sat together against the chain-link fence in the gray, predawn light, arms linked, legs touching, supported by hundreds of people who lined the road with signs

declaring *No Nukes!* and *Nuclear Weapons Should Rust in Peace.*
As the police carried us away, line after line, children and adults,
the spectators shouted their support and reminded the police,
"The Whole World Is Watching!" one of our favorite chants at
the time. On the bus, some of the police officers made eye contact with us. One or two dared a smile and I dared a smile back.
Others kept their sunglasses on, as if human connection would
just make their job harder.

Many hours later, we were released on our own recognizance. "Recognizance" immediately became one of my new
favorite words. It means recognition and awareness. We were
released to our own awareness of our own actions, the actions of
others, and our responsibility for them. I ran home to turn on the
television and watch what "the whole world" was saying about
our actions. Unfortunately, this was the same day that Prince
Charles married Princess Diana. The whole world was indeed
watching, but they were watching a wedding, not a protest.

There have been moments, such as the World Trade Organization
protests in Seattle in 1999 or the local Occupy Wall Street dem-
onstrations in 2011, when I have been part of movements where
at least some of the world *was* watching, sometimes dispassion-
ately and other times with real interest. I love the physical pleasure of connection in these moments, the feeling of power that
comes from knowing we are not alone.

I've also found this connection in moments when no one was watching, but a group of us worked together to make some small aspect of the world open to more beauty. One of my last memories of New York City is of a tea party I hosted with neighbors in a local community garden slated to be turned into a parking lot. Dressed in tea dresses and suits, we sipped tea from mismatched cups and listened to Vivaldi on a little boom box, enjoying our communion, while outside the garden fence, people rushed past and police officers stood guard.

When the Buddhist authors I work with talk about the necessity of sangha and interbeing, I relate it to these moments of working together to alleviate suffering. In those linked arms and raised voices I feel the energy and strength of one multilayered voice. I take refuge in the shared intention, like a salmon coming home to spawn with other salmon. This is part of what it means to be human: to work together, engaged in making life better for all living beings, not for the cameras that may or may not be there, but because it is the natural outcome of awareness.

The "engaged Buddhism" that Thich Nhat Hanh developed was born from a time of war in Vietnam. Ten years before I met him, Thay wrote, "When I was in Vietnam, so many of our villages were being bombed. Along with my monastic brothers and sisters, I had to decide what to do. Should we continue to practice in our monasteries, or should we leave the meditation halls in order to help the people who were suffering from the bombardment? After careful reflection, we decided to do both. We decided to go out and help people and to do so in mindfulness.

Mindfulness must be engaged. Once there is seeing, there must be acting. Otherwise, what is the use of seeing?"*

The more I observe the world, the more I can't help but be aware of the suffering and injustice in it. I am also more aware of the many different forms and practices that compassionate action can take. Protest is one form, but if my only form of action is protest, I'm missing so many daily opportunities for action. At its base, compassionate action must have compassion and insight. The history professor Cornel West puts it this way, which I think Thay would agree with: "Justice is what love looks like in public."**

I have locked arms in protest with people like the author Grace Paley, whose insight and compassion continue to inspire me every day. And I have removed my arms from those people who pushed their ideas through, who had no idea how to listen. They had the abstract knowledge of what was the right thing to do, but not the body knowledge.

As a child, I used to ask my father when the revolution would come and how to make it come faster. I was eager for the rush and the thrill of these public displays, the joy of that large evidence of our interdependence. There are moments when the most effective way to make change is to get out into the street. From Tiananmen to Tahrir Square to Zucotti Park, people have demonstrated the power of a publicly visible response to suffering. But while these moments come, the day after these moments

---

* Thich Nhat Hanh, *Peace is Every Step* (New York: Bantam Books, 1991).
** Cornel West Official Website, www.cornelwest.com/occupt_la_100711.html

still comes as well. There are hundreds of moments in any given day when compassionate action is less dramatic but no less necessary. If justice is love in public, anytime I am in public, I have the opportunity to create justice. Listening deeply to someone else's suffering, taking care of a neighbor's child, opening the door and inviting people in to eat—these are little moments of justice that add to the larger moments that come. Sometimes I think of the little moments as practice for the big moments, but the big moments are also practice for the little ones. I want to act as if I'm in a world where compassion, kindness, and the awareness of our mutual dependence is the status quo. There is no need to wait.

26. Stop Bothering Me

I'M WALKING TO MY OFFICE to work on a book on how inter-connected everyone is and how we all need each other, when a man starts yelling at me out of his car window. I'm in the cross-walk and he is driving a car, and apparently, I am walking too close to his car. "Why don't you watch where you're going, you idiot!" he yells. It's a red light, so he is stuck there, glowering at me. I stare back at him. I do not smile compassionately and think about his difficult childhood or his rough day or how he and I are intricately connected. I stand there with my arms crossed. I say, "I'm in the crosswalk, you're driving. I have the light. You're the one who should be looking where you're going."

"Oh, shut up," he says. He turns up his music. I continue to stand there, arms crossed, staring. Finally he bursts out, "Why don't you just stop bothering me!" Then he rolls up the window and the light turns green and he drives away.

We human beings are deeply reliant upon each other for survival and emotional nourishment. Babies do not thrive with-out touch. Our very existence is not possible without others. At the same time, humans cause each other a tremendous amount of irritation and pain. We cause more harm, both to other human beings and to everything on the planet, than any other species.

So how do we create sustainable and just communities when other people are also our biggest problem, so annoying at best, and brutal and dangerous at worst? It can seem that other people are the whole of the problem. But other people are the whole of the problem only if we are stuck on the idea that they are somehow separate from ourselves.

A few years ago, I was sitting in a dinner meeting with a number of monks and nuns to discuss the covers of some of Thich Nhat Hanh's books. These meetings are the opposite of our family dinners, where the floor often goes to the person who interrupts the most, gesturing wildly to make a point. In the usual Plum Village style, we sat in a circle on the floor. We invited the bell and meditated for a few moments before we began. Each person listened quietly to whoever was speaking. We joined our palms to "bow-in" if we wanted to speak, and "bowed-out" when we were finished. During the whole meeting, the monk who was taking notes kept clicking the top of his ballpoint pen. He did it while he talked; he did it while I talked; he did it while the other monks and nuns talked. I kept thinking, "Don't click it again. Don't click it again." And then, of course, he would click again.

Instead of focusing on the book covers, I was stuck trying to figure out what the problem was. Was the problem that the monk was unconsciously clicking his pen when he was supposed to be aware and calm, or was the problem that I was letting it bother me, instead of using each click as a reminder to breathe deeply? Finally I gave up. The image came uninvited to my mind of this monk as a young boy, clicking his pen in school when he was supposed to be paying attention to his math lesson. I was just as distracted as a child, but quieter—whole notebooks taken up with my doodling during chemistry. Maybe there was no problem. He was clicking his pen, I was bothered, and it was just what was happening. It was, as a young New York Zen teacher used to tell me, "just information." I could be irritated and still have empathy for this young fidgety boy-turned-monk. The words of the angry man at the crosswalk could just be information for me that here was someone having a hard time. I didn't have to take care of him and I didn't have to be bothered by him. Other people are inspirational, necessary, and sometimes irritating. We don't get to choose everyone who we come in contact with, which is a good thing. But we do get to choose, in any given moment, if and how we want to respond to them.

27. Micro Metta

IF PEOPLE ARE CAUSING REAL INJURY, I try to stop them with my words and concrete physical actions. But if people are just displeasing to me, I basically have two choices: move away from them or actively wish them well. A key Buddhist practice for wishing people well is offering *metta,* which means love, or loving kindness, in Pali. Metta is the practice of concentrating on sending people your wish that they are well. This is a serious business, not the airy greeting card kind of wishing well. In the Metta Sutta, the Buddha's teachings on love, he said, "Just as a mother loves and protects her only child at the risk of her own life, we should cultivate boundless love to offer to all living beings in the entire cosmos. Let our boundless love pervade the whole universe, above, below, and across. Our love will know no obstacles, our heart will be absolutely free from hatred and enmity. Whether standing or walking, sitting or lying, as long as we are awake, we should maintain this mindfulness of love in our own heart. This is the noblest way of living."[*]

Loving even one person in this way can be exhausting. It's difficult to genuinely wish people well if you can't figure out a way to care about them. My father asks me, "What's the point

[*] Thich Nhat Hanh, *Teachings on Love* (Berkeley, CA: Parallax Press, 2007).

of wishing people well if they irritate you? Isn't that just condescending?" But I don't wish people well in order to feel superior to them. I do it, when I can, because these difficult, challenging people are equally as important to my survival as my loved ones.

Everyone seems to do metta meditation a little differently. This one is from Deer Park Monastary, in Escondido, California. I like it because the monastics sometimes sing it to the tune of "Amazing Grace," but also because the words are simple and clear. The first offering focuses on wishing yourself well. My stepmother Arisika uses this as her birthday wish each year:

> *May I be safe and protected.*
> *May I be peaceful and at ease.*
> *May I be healthy and strong.*
> *May I be well.*

The subsequent offerings address loved ones, then people you feel neutral about, and, finally, those who challenge you, in that order:

> *May you be safe and protected.*
> *May you be peaceful and at ease.*
> *May you be healthy and strong.*
> *May you be well.*

The last metta offering is for the world.

May we be safe and protected.
May we be peaceful and at ease.
May we be healthy and strong.
May we be well.

This meditation works well in a nice calm setting, such as a re-treat or park, or even at home in a quiet room. But when I am in the thick of daily life, when someone hurts the feelings of someone I love, I often don't feel like doing metta meditation and I don't find it useful. Metta requires time and concentration and sometimes I don't have either.

I stayed stuck on this, feeling guilty that I couldn't get through an entire metta meditation, until Brother Phap Ho, a monk from Australia who now lives in Escondido, gave me a tool. He was talking about generosity, another way of describ-ing metta meditation, and he summarized the practice in just two quick questions: *But what about me?* and *But what about you?* I think of these two questions as micro metta. Since I am, like most people, prone to quick, thick, and gluey judgments, it's good to have an equally quick tool to get unstuck from them.

When someone else is irritating me, I tend to focus on him and his offending behaviors. This is the perfect time to ask myself "But what about me?" What do I need? What would I be doing if I wasn't focused on this as an obstacle? If I truly knew that this person wasn't in my way, what would I be doing? What would I be working toward? I return to my intention. My intention is why I'm here in any given moment, and it's my irritation, not the other person and what they're doing, that's the real distraction.

For the second part ("But what about you?") I imagine the other person answering this question, "But what about you?" and this lets me have the conversation in my head that I can't or don't want to have with someone directly. It reminds me that while he may still be irritating and wrong in a million different ways, I can still take a moment to imagine what is going on with him—not in order to excuse or change his behavior, or to change my own, but just to understand.

I have the kind of face that reflects the most fleeting emotions, a moment's joy or bother is telegraphed to the world and I can't take it back. I don't think I will ever have a face as serene and calm as Thay's or even one like Jason's, which projects affability even when he is supremely annoyed. I still get bothered, sometimes many times a day. But pausing for micro metta has helped me let go of my displeasure sooner, sometimes even before it furrows my brow. The irritation still comes quickly but now, almost as quickly, it goes.

28. Our Space in the Universe

ANNA WAS MY FIRST STEPMOTHER, a fierce lawyer, artist, singer, school board member, baker, restaurant owner, and single mother of a brilliant teenage daughter. She never went a day without wearing high heels and eventually had to have lifts put in her sneakers because she could no longer flatten out her foot. Anna was the first adult who was deliberately mean to me. When we met, she stood silently assessing me, from the top of my curly hair to my dirty sneakers, her hands on my shoulders. Then she sniffed, as if smelling something bad, and turned away to hug my little sister.

My sister and I moved into Anna's house when I was ten years old. The ceilings were painted gold and the walls were lined with dolls from around the world, covered in a fine layer of dust. There was a slightly off-key piano, a cramped pantry to hide in when the grown-ups fought, an old dog named Lobita with one blue eye and one white one, and a paved backyard with a single skinny flowering apple tree. Every surface at Anna's, from the kitchen table to the living room mantel to the stairs, was covered in stuff: mail, make-up, CDs, scarves, and tchotchkes of all kinds.

On weekday mornings, the five of us would squeeze into Anna's gold VW bug, her six-foot-tall daughter, my two-year-old sister, and I crammed knees-up in the back seat, Anna and my father up front. She would drive us to school while simultaneously putting on her Kohl eyeliner in the driver's side mirror and arguing with my father.

The day we moved into Anna's, I carried the thick black duffel bag that I would lug back and forth from my mother's house to Anna's each week for the next seven years. I lugged it up the stairs to my new room. As I opened the door, I was stopped by an overpowering smell. There in the middle of the carpet, right where the hallway met the bedroom, was a big pile of dog shit from Anna's dog.

I went down and whispered to my dad about the pile. We cleaned it up as best we could, but the stain remained for the rest of the years we lived there. I used to keep a small rug on top of it, but I always knew what was underneath. I spent my first night in that house with all the windows open, trying to escape the sickly sweet smell of soap and perfume used to cover up the dog shit.

Over the next eight years, Anna tried various techniques to convey her dislike of me, from not speaking to me for weeks, to accusing me of stealing hundreds of dollars, to having me scrub the kitchen counters and the stove.

Eventually, I moved out. First to my mother's house and then to college across the country. Two years later, my father moved out. I saw Anna only once after that. But when I returned to the Bay Area after fifteen years, I knew I might run into her. What would I do? What would I say? For many years, Anna was the litmus test I ran for every generalization in every Buddhist book I edited. I didn't want to feel compassion for her and didn't see any reason why I should.

Anna and I were both adults now. I no longer relied on her for shelter or food. We were equals, so I could, theoretically, wish her well. But I didn't want to put energy into it and I didn't feel like I needed to. I didn't wish her harm. That seemed good enough. She was no longer taking up any space in my universe.

I finally saw Anna one day in the deli section of the grocery store. Wearing tight black pants and balancing on red high heels, she stood in front of the refrigerated dairy products, the glass door held wide open. I stopped. Clutching my toilet paper, my tissues, and my bottle of children's vitamin C to my chest, I leaned against the aisle, not willing to be seen. I could feel my heart beating like a rabbit's and I took a few slow calm breaths. *But what about me?* In those breaths, I was surprised to notice that I was completely fine. I stayed there, enjoying my calm. She made her way to the counter, paid for her items, and walked out. I didn't wish for her wild success and I didn't have any desire to see her ever again, but I was solid enough to wish her, if not well, then well enough. *May her loved ones be safe and healthy. May her feet not hurt too much. May she get through the day without falling.*

29. Peace Talks

A LITTLE WHILE AGO, the extended commune family gathered at my friend Millie's granddaughter's house in Arcata, California, for dinner. I sat on the floor next to Millie, who I'd known since I was small. Millie's daughter-in-law, her grandson, and a few other relatives are peeling cucumbers and mashing potatoes. Millie is ninety-one. She raised three children, all of whom left the East Coast to become West Coast mountain hippies. Millie moved west to be with them and has at one time or another taken in and helped raise three grandchildren. Her daughter raises goats and horses. A logging truck killed one son. Her surviving son is an environmentalist and a songwriter. Millie and I share a baguette and a glass of wine and I tell her about the guy in the crosswalk and about how, despite all these years working for Thay and practicing sitting, I still get so mad at people.

"The trick," Millie whispered, "is not to be judgmental, either of others or yourself."

I was afraid of this. I'm incredibly judgmental. Many of us are. Studies show that most people take only 1/100th of a second, literally a blink of an eye, to decide their first impression of someone. This first impression doesn't change with longer exposure, either. This is not just how people choose whom to date or to let into their house, but who we elect to lead our country.* It makes sense that humans developed rapid-fire judgment. It was and still is necessary for our survival.

It's just that we can't seem to figure out, when we're out of immediate danger, when to hold on to our judgments and when to let them go. That is one reason to practice mindfulness. The only way to create a pause between stimulus and response is to practice awareness, and often. Martial arts and self-defense training operates on a similar understanding: If I've practiced punching someone a thousand times in a class, I'm less likely to freeze if the situation comes up on the street. Hopefully, those thousands of repetitions will hone my instinct to hit hard and run.

I remind Millie that her sharp judgment and critical thinking are two of the things I love most about her. She reminds me that there is a big difference between making judgments and holding onto them. We all make judgments and distinctions and that's natural and good. "It's when we hold onto the judgments and let them get in the way that we harm ourselves and others," she says.

Millie had a big argument with one of the caregivers at the retirement community where she lives. The woman was impatient with her and unkind words were exchanged. Afterward, Millie was so upset she couldn't sleep. She didn't like how the woman had spoken to her and she didn't like how she had responded. The next day when the caregiver came into the room, Millie expressed genuine regret for her words and asked if the

* *Science 2.0* and *Psychological Science*. Some studies suggest 1/10th of a second, but more research supports the idea that judgments formed at 1/100th of a second are the same as those formed at 1/10th.

caregiver would be willing to have a "peace talk." The caregiver said no.

So Millie had a peace talk with herself, letting the conversation that she wanted to have with the caregiver unfold in her own mind. In that conversation, the caregiver talked and talked, telling Millie about her long day and why their fight had been the final straw. Millie apologized for causing the caregiver suffering, and the caregiver apologized for her harsh words. Afterward, Millie felt much better.

Later that night, Millie was laughing, telling a funny story about her daughter's first boyfriend. I, on the other hand, was still irritated at the caregiver. What kind of person wouldn't agree to have a peace talk with a woman like Millie?

I never met the woman but later that night, after Millie had left and I'd put the kids to bed, I had more space to actually answer that question. *But what about you?* I asked and the caregiver explained about her busy day and her teenager at home, the hard physical work, and the cranky patients not thanking her or bothering to learn her name. I remembered suddenly that I'd had that job. When I first moved to Vermont after college, I worked as an aide in a home for elderly people with Alzheimer's and other forms of dementia. The work was physically exhausting, involving bending over and constantly carrying, wiping, bathing, and cleaning people who were often bewildered and angry. Besides a fifteen-minute lunch break for a quick smoke out back by the garbage cans, we were on duty from 6 AM until 2 PM or 2 PM until 10 PM. It would have been hard for even the sweetest ninety-one-year-old woman in the world to break through my level of exhaustion.

∽

I learned judgment at my father's knee, and he is probably the most judgmental person I know—as well as one of the most generous, loving, and compassionate. Osha grew up in New York City, where he lived with his father, the political scientist Franz Neumann, his mother Inge Neumann, and his stepfather, the philosopher Herbert Marcuse. The rebellious child of German Jewish refugees, intellectuals whose only religion was rationality, he left home to join the protests in the streets in the sixties, living and raging with a group called Up Against the Wall M—F—kers. They called themselves "a street gang with analysis" and became momentarily famous for throwing garbage on the steps of Lincoln Center. Still, Osha absorbed his father's teachings enough to pass them on to me. Marcuse's "Repressive Tolerance" essay, which my dad gave me as a teenager, became my guide for how to navigate questions of tolerance and acceptance:

> The tolerance expressed in [supposed] impartiality serves to minimize or even absolve prevailing intolerance and suppression. If objectivity has anything to do with truth, and if truth is more than a matter of logic and science, then this kind of objectivity is false, and this kind of tolerance inhuman.[*]

This was a revelation and a validation of what made intuitive sense to me: It was not only okay but necessary to be intolerant of what was intolerable and unjust. That intolerance, though, shouldn't take the form of passive judgment, the worst of the worst. Intolerance needs to take the form of action against the intolerable and unjust.

Every Friday, my father picks up Luna and Plum from school and we make dinner together. Sometimes, we combine forces; he chops garlic and I season the soup. Other times, we have a cook-off, each of us coming up with our own way to make lasagna, and then the family blind taste-tests the resulting steaming pans.

My father is finally slowing down his work schedule. The other day, as we were cutting onions and sautéing peppers, I asked him what he was most proud of in his fifty years of working. "It has felt good to be out in the streets day or night for people who needed it most," he said. "At the same time, I hope that I've been able to do that work while still being kind and non-judgmental." This answer surprised me, coming from the man who was currently looking down his nose at my onion-chopping technique. But this is the difference between critique and judgment. Criticism is necessary, judgment unhelpful. Even Osha, still confident in his superior lasagna, admits this. "Judgment can be such a distraction," he says as we wash up our empty pans. "It can keep you focused on someone else instead of on your own ability to change things."

*Herbert Marcuse, "Repressive Tolerance," in Robert Paul Wolff et al., *A Critique of Pure Tolerance* (Boston, MA: Beacon Press, 1997), www.marcuse.org/herbert/pubs/60spubs/65repressivetolerance.htm

30. Bringing Outsiders In

EVERY YEAR, sometime around mid-November, our kids start a campaign to become like the Joneses. Not the Rosenzweigs, the Joneses. There's no "Happy Holidays," no "Festival of Lights," no "Season's Greetings." For them, it's all about Christmas, all the time. They long to adorn our front yard in mad energy-gobbling holiday lights, to get a six-foot-tall Christmas tree you can see from the window, and to craft elaborate Christmas decorations out of recycled tin. They get up early each morning to make cards with pictures of trees and Santa. They squirrel away pieces of chalk and write "MERRY CHRISTMAS" in all caps on the sidewalk. Luna changes the elastic bands on her braces to red and green and wears only red and green hair ties. Plum, who was happy to inform the other kids that Santa isn't real, has the elaborate rationalization that "even though Santa isn't real and is just a person dressed up, the guy who dresses up and rides the sleigh and has reindeer is STILL going to come down my chimney and give me presents."

I'm not opposed to Christmas. I can belt out "Jingle Bells" with the best of them. But it never occurred to me to want, much less ask for, a tree. Or holiday lights. Or even presents. On the commune we celebrated solstice but, once in the city, we spent Christmas with close family friends who'd been raised with the whole nine yards: grandparents and presents and a big tree, eggnog and bacon and stockings. I loved it, and I loved that I got to be a peripheral part of it. For Hanukkah, we visited the downstairs neighbors who made latkes and could pronounce the Hebrew words correctly.

So my children's steadfastness in owning Christmas is startling; it may not be me, but it's them and it's their father, who grew up with Lutheran and Catholic relatives and the whole shebang. We have tried a compromised version, with a potted blue spruce that lives in the yard most of the year and comes in from the cold in mid-December. We hang their handmade decorations and a few ornaments passed down from their father's grandparents, twist white lights around the trunk, and tape a tinfoil star on top. They laugh at my determination to call this our "solstice tree."

We spend Christmas morning with the same family friends we always have, drinking eggnog and rummaging through stockings. I make sure there are little things for the stockings, toys for the kids, and possibly some handmade art for the grown-ups. But there's a part of me that still feels like a guest at someone else's strange and lovely ritual. It's not that I want my kids to exchange all their Christmas fanaticism for Hanukkah fanaticism or any other holiday extravaganza. It's not that I want to "own" Christmas or create my own hippie version of it; I like it just the way it is. It's more that I am bewildered by my children's sense of ownership, and that they think of all the holiday wrappings and lights as theirs.

~

My first sense of identity, once we moved to the city, was as an outsider. More than being a girl, a kid, a Jew, a European American, a daughter, rich, or poor, I was an outsider. That was a fine, if not always pleasurable, place to be. I'd seen more naked bodies before I was five than most people see in a lifetime. Other commune kids figured out how to "pass" once they left. Some of them became cheerleaders and football players. They joined sororities and fraternities, or went into the army. But I stayed on the outside, looking in. I didn't know how to do anything else.

It wasn't just because of my commune childhood. Outsider identity has been passed down in my family for generations. Jews and immigrants, my parents and their parents saw themselves as observers, ones who stood on the edge and looked in at the ones the country and its systems were designed for. My parents dealt with their otherness by either intellectualizing it, in my father's case, or trying to belong, in my mother's case.

My mother grew up in Mexico City and then moved to New York City, where the other kids laughed at her because she talked funny and had never heard of Jesus. Her father abandoned the family for other women, first in Venezuela and then in Israel. Her mother, Alice, stayed in New York.

Alice, the blond-haired and light-eyed daughter of Russian Jewish immigrants, was so good at passing as non-Jewish that, when she was in her seventies, her Jewish boyfriend didn't want to bring her home to meet his ninety-year-old parents because he was afraid they'd be upset at him for dating a *shiksa*. Alice was visibly disappointed by Yeshi, her dark-haired, darker-skinned daughter. My mother grew up with the idea that you should try to belong to whatever group is getting the best treatment. As we snuck into first-class lines, private events, and clubs we couldn't afford, she would assure us that we belonged there. She didn't want to miss out on anything so we celebrated every holiday with whatever people knew how to do it right. We went to Catholic Mass, Nouruz, Three Kings Day, and Orisha and Ramadan celebrations. Passover was a long hungry evening, mostly in Hebrew, at the home of Jewish friends who knew all the words. Christmas at our friends' home was done perfectly, with a wreath, stockings, a huge tree, presents, and a fireplace with cookies and milk.

Being an observer meant that I was rarely bored and often restless. We had to stay alert, learn how things were done, and work hard to fit in. But my kids don't feel the need to pass or to work really hard to deserve Christmas. They feel entitled to all its joy and glitz, without effort and they are determined not to miss a single sparkle.

One recent winter night, I came home late and saw our blue spruce sparkling with white lights through the window. It disoriented me. Could that house be mine, with that tree visible from the street? Was it advertising our allegiance to the majority over the minority, to the insider over the outsider, to the many over the few? Would my children really learn compassion, empathy, and critical discourse if they grew up with that tree?

Then I thought of my partner, Jason, one of the most hands-down compassionate people I know. Growing up working-class in rural Washington State, an artist among football players, he too always identified with the underdog, the weirdo, and the kid sitting alone in the corner. It seems most people do, at least at one time or another.

My children have a net of economic security that, while quite thin, is much more than many families have. And yet they will struggle, because we all do. They will also feel included and connected in a different way than I do. But the question is not what they will feel, but what they will make of that feeling. Their insistence on the twinkling lights is a needed reminder: Compassion and empathy can come as much from our sense of belonging to a larger humanity as it can from our sense of otherness. This is another way of thinking of interbeing. We are thrown into this world together and can only thrive if we can find the ways that we are connected to the whole.

31. It's a Great Life If You Don't Weaken

FOR BUDDHISTS, a sangha is a community that practices mindfulness together. My sangha, my community, is a group of people who take care of each other and each other's children, giving what they can and getting what they need, whether or not they call what they are doing mindfulness. And any community needs a place to gather. Thich Nhat Hanh has his monasteries, Yeshi has her shared house at the beach, and Osha has his legal clinic, open to whomever wanders in needing help. The closest thing Jason and I have to a gathering place is our small home. We do our best to model it after the home of our friend, Cynthia, who died a couple of months ago at the age of ninety-five.

The first time I came to Cynthia's home, atop a cliff in the Carmel Highlands on the California central coast, I couldn't have been more than six years old. Cynthia was an emissary from a whole different world: a traditional British Anglo-Saxon world where children were left to run free outdoors and behaved themselves indoors. There was a parrot in the garden, and there were ducks in the pond, chickens and dogs, and hundreds of wonderful trees and bushes for playing hide-and-seek. There were tire swings and tricycles and secret paths to the beach. Inside, there was a well-used couch with a bin of comic books hidden behind it. From *Mad* magazine and Archie and Sabrina, I learned that gas prices had gone through the roof and that when you're a teenager and you like somebody, you should never tell them directly. From Cynthia, I learned that the key to a long life was a banana and a glass of hot water with lemon every morning.

At Cynthia's there was a tea cozy covering a warm pot of black tea, a set of worn playing cards, and a tin filled with cookies that could be sneaked in the night without consequence—as long as you didn't take the last one. Cynthia was the kind of older woman I'd always hoped to meet, but thought existed only in books. She was a combination of Mrs. Piggle-Wiggle and Mary Poppins, without any nonsense. Cynthia was brusque but loving; practical, yet a big lover of the bustle of children and community and celebration. She drew all kinds of people, and their friends, to her home, and her sense of how to observe various traditions was flawless. From Thanksgiving to Easter, she knew how to make a ritual work with just the right balance of structure and free time for hanging out and eating. Cynthia and I shared a belief in aloe vera as the cure for sunburns, an interest in baseball as long as the Oakland A's were playing, and a firm understanding that tradition grounds a person and that consistency is a necessary safe harbor.

I emulate Cynthia where I can. I like my hot water with lemon and keep the comic book section well stocked. I try, with sporadic success, to follow her "waste not, want not" credo and think of her each time I force myself to wash out our plastic bags.

And we fill our home with people, both friends and friends of friends. We have friends we share dinner with every Wednesday night, including any of their or our extended family who happen to be in town, and we have an open-door policy on my dad's Friday night dinners: anyone can come over as long as they bring some food or drink to share.

Cynthia, and my mom as well, often rented a room to friends or well-referenced strangers to help pay the bills. If someone needed a room and couldn't pay, they stayed for free. In our house, there is almost always someone staying in the back room. These friends and friends of friends come from China, Poland, and Gambia as well as across the United States and have expanded our relationship to the world.

All this makes for lots of voices and lots of dishes, and our little house fills up quickly. But usually there are enough cooks and cleaners that it actually makes life easier and I can retreat to the couch, listening to the voices with my eyes closed, until a kid comes and tells me she needs to go to bed.

I've found that what I suspected as a child was true: It can be isolating and exhausting living in your own house with just your own family and your own work to do. It's somehow easier when there are others to help cook and clean and the kids rove as a pack, whirlwinding through our house but then moving on to the next house, so that I find myself unexpectedly and blissfully alone for a moment. Cynthia liked to say, "It's a great life if you don't weaken." I do weaken, and often, but at least our home is full enough that there will likely be friends around to catch me when I fall.

32. Make Fewer Strangers

WHEN MY SISTER GOT MARRIED, Plum and Luna became very interested in the process by which a former stranger becomes part of the family. They know there was a time, not too long ago, when there were racial restrictions on whom people could marry in this country and they know that, in most states, a person can't marry someone of the same sex. Both kids are firm believers that people should marry whomever they want, as long as they're nice and don't mind that you still want to live with your mother. "Can you marry a stranger?" they want to know. Yes, I tell them, but it's not advisable. "Can you marry someone and not live with them?" "Can you marry someone who speaks a different language or is from a different planet?" Yes, I tell them, you can marry whomever you want. "Then can I marry someone in my family?" Plum asks, giving Luna a speculative eye.

No, I explain, you can't. Part of the reason you marry someone is to expand your family and start a new one. "But Ericka and Eric are married and they're family," Plum says, referring to the parents of one of her closest friends. Yes, I explain, but they weren't a family when they decided to get married. You make a family, I explain to them, not just by marrying, but by being connected to each other and taking care of each other. We make our family larger so we can expand who we are and so we can make fewer strangers.

My attempt to turn most people I meet into my community and to enlarge our definition of family is probably in part because I don't have a large biological family. The relatives who didn't die in the Second World War died not long afterward, or else didn't have many children or didn't keep in touch with the family members they left behind in Russia, Germany, and Poland. By the time I was old enough to look around, our relatives were down to one aunt and one grandfather, Herbert, whom I loved dearly. When I went to visit him in San Diego, taking the plane alone, he and my aunt would come meet me at the gate. They would drive me straight to the beach, not stopping at home first. When we got there, Herbert would hold my hands and we'd walk down to the shore where he would yell at the waves, with fake incredulity, "Are you *mad*?" For some reason I would find this unbearably funny and so he would do it again and again. Later, we would sit together in stiff-backed chairs in the hallway and, small color television on, watch the opening shot of the huge wave on the show *Hawaii Five-O*. I never questioned why the television was in the hallway or what he meant when he yelled at the waves. He died when I was ten, so I never got to ask.

My aunt, my mother's sister, who taught me how to play canasta, never had children, and died at fifty. My father's brother had quickly after college washed his hands of all things associated with the United States and moved to Canada. My mother had one other relative we saw once at a wedding, though I never figured out how exactly we were related. That was it for relatives. No wonder I was taking applications for new family members.

But my desire for fewer strangers was also in part a response to the "stranger danger" anxiety I experienced when we moved to the city. The balance between politeness, openness, wariness, and self-defense is pretty wobbly, especially for young girls. I teach my daughters to be polite, to answer questions, look people in the eye, and speak when they're spoken to. I also teach them the power of shouting and of a well-placed jab to the eyes. I want them to know how to run fast when they need to defend themselves, and when in danger not to be afraid of hurting other people's feelings or, if necessary, their bodies. I want them to be open to new people, but at the same time to rely on that blink-of-an-eye survival judgment.

On the commune, there was no such thing as a stranger. Anyone coming down the road for the first time might be greeted with a naked hug or a pistol, depending on whom they saw first. If they made it past the driveway, they were allowed to stay on a trial basis. As long as they weren't creepy, participated in meetings and did their dishes, they usually could stay as long as they wanted.

One of my strongest memories of moving to the city was my amazement at the sheer numbers of strangers I saw. Every single day, I saw people I didn't know, going about their separate lives, completely unaware of me, my parents, and my whole world. At first, we lived with a large number of families. Then we moved into a house with just one other family with two daughters, and the three of us girls would climb onto our roof and, inspired by Harriet the Spy, spend whole days writing down our observations about the people who walked past. One time, when I was about ten, the other family's daughter and I walked a few blocks to the main street and started interviewing strangers about their lives, their favorite colors and foods, and their children's names. For this, I got in trouble. "You can't go up and just talk to strangers you don't know," my dad said. "It's not safe." I stopped talking to people I didn't know. I didn't stop being interested in them.

This was the early eighties, crime was high, there were robberies in the neighborhood, and there was a particularly heightened stranger anxiety in the air. I was constantly hearing stories of little girls being pulled into cars with darkened windows. I would take the bus to school and run the three blocks home, sure that the car driving up the street was trying to kidnap me.

Plum is just now becoming aware of all the strangers around her. Each time we get in the car, she watches the people going by and says, "They don't know where we're going, right?" The other day she was leaning back, sucking on a throat lozenge that was giving her immense satisfaction, and watching the purple flowers fall from the tree outside our window. Occasionally, people would walk past. After a gaggle of teenagers sauntered by, Plum sat up abruptly. "Those people don't even know what I have in my mouth," she said. They don't, I agreed, and we don't know what they have in their mouths either.

The other day, she had her biggest revelation yet. Plum was holding my hand, staring at all the people rushing to their various jobs and appointments, when she said, "Mama! Those people don't even know if you're my mom or if you're somebody else's mom." This one upset her slightly. There were people out there who might see me walking down the street and not immediately know I was Plum's mom.

As a writer, strangers are my bread and butter, as well as my joy. I love the way that, despite the patterns and parallels, people continue to surprise me. When I moved to the Bay Area to work for Thich Nhat Hanh after so many years in New York, I missed my friends, but it was the strangers I missed most. In New York, there are always strangers to talk to and remind me of our interdependence. In the Bay Area, there were fewer people on the street, fewer communal public spaces. From the sidewalk to the grocery store to the BART train, people were more protective of their personal space. In such a place, it's easy to forget how intrinsically connected we are to others.

As with dark chocolate and red wine (in moderation), community has now also been vindicated by doctors as a health choice. Having fewer strangers around helps us live longer. "A familiar friend calms and equilibrates, mops up the cortisol spills that can weaken the immune system, and in so doing may help lengthen life—in baboons, humans, and other group-minded kinds" says science writer Natalie Angier.[*] This is not what propels me towards other people, but it makes sense. Scientifically as

[*] Natalie Angier, "The Spirit of Sisterhood Is in the Air and on the Air," *New York Times*, April 24, 2012.

well as philosophically, we are interconnected, and the more we acknowledge this, the happier we are.

One day after I'd been in the Bay Area for a year or so, I wandered into a grocery store. A woman had set up a table offering free samples of sugar-free, gluten-free, vegan, whole-grain organic cookies. The dispirited brown lumps were a hard sell, even for free, so I took pity and tried one. They were edible. To help her out, I turned to the first stranger I saw, a woman on my left. "Try these!" I said, gesturing to the table. "They've got nothing bad in them and they taste okay." The woman looked down at the little brown lumps and shuddered. "Sorry," she said, shaking her head. "I only eat raw foods."

Joanna Macy taught me a good trick for welcoming the less familiar and less-easy of strangers. In her book, *Pass it On*, she tells the story of staying in a small village in Northern India and her initial discomfort in making eye contact with the day laborers carrying heavy loads up the hills. She saw the same person each morning and the sight of him always produced such feelings of guilt and embarrassment that Joanna would look away without speaking. Then, one evening, a Tibetan nun gave a talk in which she said: "So countless are sentient beings, and so many their births throughout time, that each at some point was your mother."[*] Remembering this allowed Joanna to greet the laborer directly, to say good morning, and to keep walking. It helps me

---

[*]Joanna Macy, *Pass It On: Five Stories that Can Change the World* (Berkeley, CA: Parallax Press, 2010).

move from scorn or pity to empathy. Every other human being, from the raw food-only woman in the grocery store, to the man yelling at me from his car window, to the day laborer, could be my mother.

As a parent, I remind myself of this as well: If we are all interconnected, each of these people could also be my child. This is reason enough to want to make fewer strangers. Once, when Luna was five and Plum was two, we attempted a rare dinner out at a local restaurant a little too late in the evening. Something small, a misplaced elbow or a sharp word, set them both off and soon, waiting for our food, we had two children down on the floor, screaming and crying. As we hustled to get out of there, other patrons stared at us. Some looked at us with kindness and others with undisguised disdain. I heard one of them say to his friend, "Thank God those are not *my* children."

I had, both before and after having my own children, thought nearly the same thing when watching some young person whack another, or whine, or scream bloody murder. But then I remember that the screaming child could be my child, and sometimes *is* my child. I vow to approach them with empathy, clarity, and compassion. I remember my vow to make fewer strangers and to view the strangers who remain as my larger community I have yet to know.

33. A Marshmallow by Any Other Name

The shower drain. The picnic cups. My electric kettle, my kids' barettes, hair elastics, and toothbrushes. The earphones in my ear and the music player they are attached to. My glasses, my broom, and my cell phone.

Sometimes, the best argument for making fewer strangers are the strangers themselves. I am preparing our guest room for Caijun and her son, Lingyang, who are coming from Beijing to live with us for three weeks, and I keep tripping over things made in China.

The sponge I wash the dishes with. The Connect Four game the kids were playing. My computer. My daughter's American Girl doll.

Caijun and Lingyang are coming to study and learn English. They've been to New Haven, where an uncle teaches at Yale, and to Florida. Their email says they are fine with yogurt for breakfast. As I clean, I notice I'm speaking Spanish to Caijun and Lingyang in my head. Growing up in California, with a mom who grew up in Mexico, I automatically switch to Spanish when English won't do. It's the only other language I have.

Soap bottle, sponges, dustpan, stereo. My warm coat that says "Daughters of the Liberation" on the label. The box of picnic forks and spoons. Not my bamboo chopsticks; those are made in the United States.

I am scrubbing the bathroom and thinking of all my stereotypes. I am hoping they will not mind that our house has only one bathroom or that our family can be noisy in the mornings. I'm wondering where my assumptions come from, what movies or books or observations are coming together. I have been to Beijing once, for the U.N. World Conference on Women. I helped teach two classes, one on self-defense and one on communication. It rained the whole time, and I ate delicious eggplant, and I remember everything being very close together and cold, and that there were a lot of police officers.

As I clean up, I come across the large collection of books that Thay and I have made together and he has signed. A few of these books, one with full-color illustrations, were printed in China. A few of them were printed in South Korea, the Chinese printers having rejected them for not meeting government printing guidelines. The content was too subversive, we were told, too potentially supportive of the people of Tibet. I leave the books where they are.

My camera. My sneakers. The pen I was writing with. My plastic bankcard. The picture book I am putting away.

When I get to the train station to pick up our guests, I restrain myself from yelling out, "Hola!" Eventually, we find each other. We exchange smiles, a few words. When we get to the house, I make them tea, show them where the bathroom is, and leave them to get settled.

I wake the next morning to find Caijun sweeping our living room. I swept the day she arrived, but the pile she has collected is embarrassingly large and full of unidentifiable fluff that I missed on my first round. We smile at each other. I scurry out of the house.

Later that night, we are looking at pictures. It turns out that Caijun was a volunteer at the World Conference on Women when I was in Beijing in 1995. That night we all make pizza for dinner, my father at the helm. As Lingyang puts flour on his hand, he smiles. "I know this," he says. Every culture seems to have some dish where you shape dough and put some filling in it. We all throw the dough around without hitting the floor until it works and add the toppings. Then everyone retreats to doing their own thing until dinner is ready.

More guests arrive. Berta, who used to work taking care of Plum, has come to dinner with her husband and their six-week-old baby. Berta crossed into the United States from Guatemala at sixteen, when it was no longer safe to stay in her home village. She petitioned to stay in the United States but her petition was denied and she is now, after six years here, facing possible deportation. Her appeal is currently in the courts. We sit down, all nine of us, with our three languages and our many stories.

Politics and economics do not, of course, disappear. Lingyang and his mother pay money to stay with us and I used to pay Berta every week to take care of my daughter while I went to work at a desk. All the choices we've had and didn't have sit with us at the table tonight. We pass food, we nod and smile at each other, and watch the beautiful sleeping baby.

After dinner, we roast marshmallows on shishkabob skewers over the fire in the fireplace. We discuss the word for marshmallow in English, Chinese, and Spanish. Jason and Berta's husband talk about work, where they have some overlap. Then Berta's baby wakes, is passed around, and her cuteness admired until she's had enough and Berta puts her back to sleep. It's peaceful here for a moment in the firelight, with our sticky fingers and full bellies. There's a lull, a break from all the navigation, anxieties, and negotiation. Our differences are still there, but our awareness shifts, and there is a meeting point, a loosening of our attachments to our views, an awareness of our interconnectedness. Community, like awareness itself, is a balance. The present moment is never only joy or only suffering. To turn strangers into community requires holding an understanding of both our differences and our connection.

The baby wakes again. Berta and her family go back out into the night, Caijun and Lingyang return to their room, and I grab a sponge to wipe the marshmallow off the living room table. We return to the illusion of our separate selves and separate worlds, but with skin a little more porous.

34. Wanting It All

I WENT BACK TO WORK for Thich Nhat Hanh when Luna was six weeks old. I had planned, as most parents do, to have an easy baby, one who would sleep peacefully while I edited. No one would even notice she was there. I didn't have that kind of baby. Luna was quiet when she was sleeping, but she only liked to sleep if she was in motion. She could burst into explosive screams at any moment and generally howled for an hour or two, from 7 to 9 in the evening, no matter how much she had slept before, what I ate, or where we were.

I took out a couple of the cardboard boxes in my attic office and put in a little baby hammock. I replaced my chair with a big bouncy ball so she and I could bounce while I worked. I kept a stroller at the ready outside. When she was about to let loose a large cry, I would rush her outside for a little walk. This worked, in that my coworkers thought Luna was quiet and well behaved, while out on the street everyone we passed thought she was a wild beast.

I mastered the art of typing one-handed while I nursed and got to know most of the shopkeepers in the neighborhood. The best part was when I had meetings in my office. I would sit on the ball as we discussed whatever topic was at hand and, whenever I spoke, everyone's eyes would follow the up-and-down motion of the ball, and they would find themselves nodding along with whatever I said. There was a lot of harmonious agreement at those meetings.

Luna learned to crawl in that office, at which point I either needed to come up with a different plan or get a much bigger office with a jungle gym. Luna started staying home with various friends, family, and caretakers while I was at work, and I began the juggling and running back and forth so familiar to many working mothers. I don't think I necessarily worked better with her gone. My head just filled with to-do lists. I wished I had, if not Luna, some other small child nearby, to force me to walk around the block or clear my head before returning to the words on the page.

With two kids, my volunteer work doing teen writing workshops, writing, and a full-time job, if I don't have a regular mindfulness practice, I teeter between isolation and overload. It's lovely when I get time to just be home with my daughters, no rushing anywhere, no plans. But if I'm home for days at a time with just them for company, I get restless. It's not that I want to get away from them, it's that I want to be around them *and* other people, including other adults.

I'm most at home in that mix that contains the whole world, adults, children, trees, babies, and goats. That means that I am working to create a community that isn't full of "play dates" or even "work time," but a life that just flows with all of these things. Perhaps I'm idealizing the *zocalo*, the village square where everyone watches everyone else's children and gardens and paints and has conversations at the same time. I know there would still be hurts and resentments and misunderstandings, but all of it would take place in a large public space.

This morning, Plum woke up at first light and called for me. We were staying at my mother's house. When I came into the room, I nuzzled her curls. She smelled like a wet cat. Her voice thick with sleep and snot and the sadness of a dream, she asked, "Did you say you were going to work today?"

"No," I said, "I'm staying with you." With that, she let herself return to a fragile sleep until the light was too bright to ignore. Then we got up together and went into the kitchen to greet the day.

There are moments, like this morning, when it is enough to be with my children in the beauty of the gray light, with the waves crashing and foaming white, the turkey vultures soaring gracefully, and the bright blue sky layered with dark clouds and fog.

And there are moments in each day, no matter how beautiful the sky or sweet-smelling my girls, when it is not enough and I long to escape and have only my words and my work. I want to move and talk fast, without waiting for anyone to catch up. I want to follow my own urgency without being swayed by the need for a snack, a nap, or a Band-Aid.

According to many surveys of working mothers, we're all striving for balance,[*] but I don't want balance. I don't want mod-

***

[*]Pew Research Center Publications, "Few Mothers Prefer Full-time Work, from 1997 to 2007," July 12, 2007, http://pewresearch.org/pubs/536/working-women. About fifty percent of working mothers say their ideal situation is part-time work, as opposed to staying at home (thirty percent) or working full-time (twenty percent).

eration and I most definitely don't want compartmentalization. Instead of an hour for getting the kids to school and then a few hours for work, and then ten minutes for snuggling before dinner and bedtime, I'd like all sorts of kids running in and out, playing over in one corner of the field while I'm writing and organizing in another. I can look up and see them whenever I need to and they can come over whenever they need to. I just want us all to follow our own rhythms enough to discover what they are.

Is this what some pundits are referring to when they say that women want it all? It's hard to imagine anyone wanting less than "it all." It doesn't seem any more selfish than wanting "balance." I don't want to live in a culture where work and children are such separate spheres that we try to pretend one sphere doesn't exist when we enter the other. Before I had kids, I thought they would expand my connection to other people. They have. I promised myself I'd be vigilant against the sneaking assumption that my children were somehow more important than any other parents' children in the world. I have. At the same time, being able to intimately know these two amazing beings, among all the amazing beings out there, has felt like a rare privilege, rather than a selfless sacrifice. Taking care of children, whether mine, those in my extended family, or those of my friends, continues to be both supremely satisfying and also limiting, precisely because it is done in such a narrowly circumscribed circle. Within it, I nourish myself and them without much distinction. Then, renewed, I am eager to go out into the larger world and engage with it, ideally with my children by my side or at least across the field where I can see them when I look up.

35. Tiny Changes at the Last Minute

I RARELY DO ANYTHING, whether it's take a deep breath or reach out to my neighbor, because I should. If I do things only out of obligation, I feel put upon, guilty, and defensive. But the idea has started to settle in that other people, even the difficult ones, are necessary. Together we will determine our collective survival.

I'm at the sink washing the dishes, my shirt soaking wet where my belly touches the rim. I'm looking out at the black crows roosting on the neighbor's roof and thinking that life is harder than it needs to be, here in this neighborhood, in this city, in this country.

In an effort to change humankind's destructive course, I'm trying to make tiny changes at the last minute. For example, this week, I tried not to add any more plastic to our house. None. I just wanted to go a week without buying plastic. That seemed relatively easy. We don't buy much plastic to start out with. But it proved impossible. I needed batteries, and they only came in a container with a hard plastic cover. We needed groceries. I had brought our own cloth bags for putting the groceries in but forgot to bring my own plastic bags for the bulk items. Should I not buy oatmeal, or not buy it in bulk, and instead buy the more expensive tin made out of other nonrenewable resources, or should

I just use a new plastic bag already? Then there's the problem of yogurt. All the yogurt seems to come in plastic containers, which we already have ten thousand of at home. Sometimes we make our own yogurt, and salsa, and hummus, but then someone gets sick or busy and nothing gets made at all.

I know this is a small thing, something most people don't have the time or resources to worry over, and something that, even if we all stopped using plastic bags today, wouldn't radically alter our CO_2 emissions.[*] But still, I just want to fix something, without having to organize or call a meeting, and I'm wondering why it's hard to do even this one small thing. Sometimes it seems like the tiny changes don't work. Can I just throw this whole urban life out the window and start over somewhere else?

So I stop washing the dishes and sit down on the kitchen chair in my damp shirt. I breathe. This is when I remember: If I believe that my only two choices are to fix things by myself or start a whole homemade revolution in the isolated mountains then I'm screwed, because neither is right for me. I'm still responsible and I can't just do "my part" because "my" part isn't separate from the whole.

It was ten in the morning in New York City on September 11, 2001, right after the collapse of the twin towers but before we knew if World War III was on its way. I huddled with friends in an Upper West Side apartment, watching the news and waiting for Jason. Jason worked a block away from the towers and had watched the second plane explode, and then walked the seventy blocks north to the apartment where I was waiting. I left the apartment only to make a quick trip to the corner store to buy water, peanuts, and chocolate. The little market was crowded with panicked folks stocking up on whatever they considered necessities, trying to get enough for themselves and their loved ones, but not wanting to hoard. Everyone was wearing a wan smile. We were stricken and vulnerable, embarrassed, scared, and heartbroken. It seemed impossible that we had ever thought other things important.

That evening, a taxi driver gave us a free ride back to our home in Brooklyn. Our neighbors and friends had gathered on our roof, where there was an inappropriately beautiful sunset mingling with the smoke still coming from where the towers used to be. We sat close together, wanting some part of our bodies—even if only a foot or an elbow—to be touching someone else's. When a friend went down to get a sweater, I waited anxiously for her to come back up. We stayed late on that roof, long after dark. We didn't know what was coming next and no one wanted to face the morning alone.

The edges of that feeling returned to me ten years later in the days following the earthquake, tsunami, and nuclear reactor meltdown in Japan in March of 2011. Since the feeling that I can't do anything is the worst feeling of all, I baked furiously to

*Fiona Hawley, "World Headed for Irreversible Climate Change in Five Years, IEA Warns," The Guardian, November 9, 2011, http://www.guardian.co.uk/environment/2011/nov/09/fossil-fuel-infrastructure-climate-change.

contribute to bake sales for the Japanese people, and then went searching for potassium iodide and seaweed for my children, in case of radiation fallout coming to Northern California. The stores were all out of any radiation-reducing herbs and supplements due to the many Bay Area folks who had panicked more quickly and efficiently than I had. But everyone at the pharmacy was warm and fragile, with wan smiles and tight voices I recognized from that day in New York.

I was struck by the flimsiness of what I was holding when I walked out of the store: blue tape to seal the windows and a brown bottle full of nettle extract. We've been trained to think that consumption (both what we buy and what we eat) is the way out of any problem. I want it to be true that if I buy enough reusable containers and stop using plastic, we will save the atmosphere. It's true, that the United States' excessive consumption of energy, electricity, and other resources is part of the problem. But the small bag of tape and herbs were just talismans and not any real protection against the earth moving, a wall of water, or the collapse of steel and concrete. People in Japan consume more than 12 milligrams of healthy iodine a day, a fifty-fold greater amount than those of us in the United States. On average, they eat more seaweed and get more exercise and live longer than people almost anywhere in the world.* In the Bay Area, per-

* Meredith Melnick, "Japanese Longevity—How Long Will It Last?" *Time Healthland*, September 5, 2011, http://healthland.time.com/2011/09/05/japanese-longevity-%E2%80%94-how-long-will-it-last/ ; Theodore T. Zava and David T. Zava, "Assessment of Japanese Iodine Intake Based on Seaweed Consumption in Japan: A Literature-based Analysis," *Thyroid Research* 4 (2011), 14, www.thyroidresearchjournal.com/content/4/1/14.

haps more than other places, it's easy to be duped into thinking that healthy eating or regular yoga practice are something moral, some kind of karmic guarantee against natural disasters, poverty, misery, or death. It's possible that, barring all kinds of natural disasters and all random acts of violence, my daily kale habit will add a few healthy seconds to my life. But a greater truth is this: We can affect our life's quality but not its quantity; its length is almost completely out of our control.

From 9/11 and Hurricane Katrina in the United States to the earthquake in Haiti and the Japanese tsunami, it was not people's emergency kits, physical condition, or hand-cranked radio that was the key to their survival, though these things certainly helped. After every disaster, researchers have found that friends and neighbors, community, is what help people survive and rebuild.* So I continue to invite the neighbors in, the easy ones and the hard ones. We drink nettle tea and look out my untaped windows, breathing and riding the waves of joy and sadness as they rise and fall.

*Shankar Vedantam, "The Key To Disaster Survival? Friends and Neighbors," *NPR*, July 4, 2011, www.npr.org/2011/07/04/137526401/the-key-to-disaster-survival-friends-and-neighbors.

Epilogue: A Million Present Moments

I SOMEHOW THOUGHT that in ten years of working daily with Zen masters, Buddhist priests, mindfulness teachers, psychologists, and other trained experts, I would have learned something about staying in the present moment. But after all this time, the present moment is still a hard place for me to hang out in for long, probably because just when I think I've gotten used to it, it changes.

I finally took a trip alone to Deer Park Monastery in Southern California. Thich Nhat Hanh wasn't there. I didn't have an editorial or business meeting with any monks and nuns. In fact, I recognized as I drove up, that it was my first trip to Deer Park, or to any retreat center or monastery, that wasn't for work.

I felt lost at first without kids or a meeting or too many things to do. Retreatants and monastics walked slowly past me, moving from the lotus pond to the Dharma Hall to the eating area. Left foot lift, inhale, step, breathe. Right foot lift, inhale, step, breathe.

I left the main center and took a walk up to a stupa on the mountain. I'd seen it many times before, but only when I'd looked up as I walked from one scheduled appointment to the next. The dirt path was bumpy and dusty. Amid the desert beauty there were rusting soda cans and plastic rings. I lost the trail and ended up going through the brush before arriving at the little stone hut. It was empty, but cleanly swept and a fresh flower still lay on a small altar. Experimentally, hesitantly, I sat down. No one was watching. I didn't have any place to be. I closed my eyes. I didn't try to find any peace. I just sat there. Practicing. I felt strangely vulnerable, as if I was about to be caught betraying some ideal.

After a few moments, I opened my eyes. The hut looked the same. I walked down the hill and slowly the voices of the monastery came up to meet me. With their voices, I felt the slow wave of judgment, thought, and anxiety rise in me. I started to hurry up, to walk faster, and then I did something I rarely do. I slowed down. I stopped walking and just stood in the path. I can always come home, I reminded myself and I closed my eyes.

You can, at any moment, come home to yourself. I have probably written, rewritten, or edited some version of this phrase of Thich Nhat Hanh's hundreds of times. But this, standing in the road, was the practice.

One of the reasons I've been so reluctant all these years to close my eyes is because I can't bear to miss out on anything. I'm often rushing late to something and leaving early to get to the next thing. I want to arrive, as Thay says, in the present moment, and I'd like to look put together when I get there. But the hazard of being everywhere is that in the process my shirt gets stained, my hair falls out of its clip, and my coat matches nothing but my underwear. Even when I get home, I often forget to "come home."

I keep jumping up to look around and make sure I haven't missed something that's happening outside the window. It's not material greed. I don't need to have it all; I just want to experience it all.

It's true that I want to approach life eyes open and arms wide, but to do this right I also need to be able to close my eyes. Other people will still be there. Coming home to myself doesn't mean that I am alone.

When I come back from Deer Park, winter has settled into a gray fog over the Bay Area. Jason and I take the kids to my mom's at Muir Beach for winter solstice. Luna puts on her pajamas at three in the afternoon and is determined to stay in them for the rest of the day. The rest of us follow suit because being warm and cozy and drinking hot chocolate is our winter solstice family tradition.

We settle in to ourselves and our home, burrowing into the early darkness. We wrap ourselves in blankets and listen to the wind and the waves and talk about the Earth tilting away from the sun here in the Northern Hemisphere. Jason jumps up to make a model that shows how in the upper reaches of Alaska, where his cousins live, this is a day without light, yet our friends in New Zealand will be allowed to play until late in the evening because this is their sunniest day. And although we can't feel the Earth's tilt, I believe in it and can picture it in my mind. The darkness of the night is indisputable. The need for friends, warm food, and light is elemental. The orange circles the grapefruit in the makeshift solar system that Jason has created on the floor and I know that, starting tomorrow, each day will be a little longer and a little lighter.

Practices

BEING AVAILABLE

1) Begin during a relatively quiet time. One easy way to practice is with your phone, if you carry one or have one at work, because it probably rings throughout the day. When the phone rings, take a breath and listen to the first ring as a question rather a command. On the other end, someone is asking "Are you available?" Inhale and exhale slowly while it rings and decide in that moment if you have the attention to answer it. There are some moments when your answer will be no. In those moments, don't answer.

2) Give yourself a physical way of checking your availability when you are busy. Some people do this naturally, but if you don't, there are plenty of unobtrusive ways to physically check in with yourself. You can try putting a finger on your wrist, or curling and uncurling of your toes, or making any subtle movement that is accompanied by asking yourself the question, "Are you available?"

3) Ask other people if they are available before you engage with them and notice their response. Sometimes, people are wary at first. Why are you asking? What do you want from them? If you are asking someone else, don't ask them if they're available for a specific task, such as "Are you available to wash the dishes?" The question is "Are you available for any more input? Can you give me your full attention in this moment?" They might say no.

SETTING YOUR INTENTION

1) Do this at the same time every morning, ideally when you first wake up. Inhale and exhale with awareness. *Breathing in, I know I am breathing in. Breathing out, I know I am breathing out.* No matter what else is going on in your life, you will be taking a first awake breath of the morning as long as you are alive, so you might as well make it a conscious one. It won't take any more time and could not possibly hurt.

2) Set your day's intention. This is not the same as your to-do list. It also doesn't have to be a big, life ambition type intention, although if you know what that is, it can certainly be connected to it. The key thing is not

to worry too much whether you've got the right intention for that day. Just ask yourself the question and see how it is to follow through on whatever it is you pick. Start small: to smile at the person who annoys you or to listen deeply for five minutes to someone that you love. It could be to move more slowly or to speak more clearly. It can be to stop a few times during the day or to engage in one compassionate act. The desired outcome can stay the same or change from day to day, but your intention to practice awareness stays constant

BEING WITH PAIN AND SUFFERING

1) Pain will come. Prepare yourself by practicing mindful breathing when you don't feel severe pain. Bring your awareness to every part of your body that doesn't hurt. Even if your pain isn't physical, remembering the physical parts of your body that work well can be a comfort. I've adapted this from Thay's basic breathing exercise to focus on what works well. Modify it in a way that works for you.

Breathing in, I am aware of the working parts of my body.
Breathing out, I am thankful for what works.

2) Pain isn't personal. We often wonder why we feel the pain and what we did to cause it. But pain will come no matter what we do. Instead of trying to avoid it or fight it off, we can do what we can to lessen the arrow's sting.

Breathing in, I know that pain comes and goes.
Breathing out, I let it go.

3) There are always conditions for happiness around us. This doesn't negate or lessen the challenge of either acute or chronic pain; just that happiness and beauty are also present, even if they seem irrelevant or hard to identify.

Breathing in, I am aware of one small thing of beauty.
Breathing out, I am thankful for that beauty.

4) Impermanence is a reality, both when things are hard and also when they are good.

Breathing in, I feel this pain.
Breathing out, I know it will pass.

MICRO METTA

1) Micro metta works best if you practice it first in a neutral moment, when you are not either enamored or irritated. Morning is a good time for this, because asking yourself, *But what about me?* in the morning can be a way of setting your intention for the day. What do you need, either emotionally or materially, so that you can approach this day with clarity, compassion, and kindness? A cup of tea? Five minutes of meditation? If you have what you need, then other people's confusions and irritations are just their confusions and irritations, and you see more clearly that they are not personally meant for you.

2) Breathing in, ask yourself, *But what about me?* Breathing out, don't rush to answer. If your mind wanders, ask yourself again.

3) If you are practicing in the morning, bring your mind to someone who you know you will see during the day or interact with in some way. Just pick one person. If you won't see anyone that day, pick someone who

you won't see but who is affecting you at that moment, maybe a person whom you want to help or a person whose actions are upsetting you. In the setting of daily life, you probably won't have time to get to the whole world, so just pick one.

4) Breathing in, ask yourself, *But what about you?* Breathing out, don't rush the answer. If your mind wanders, ask yourself again. If nothing comes, imagine this person as your parent and ask again. Imagine this person as your child, and ask again.

5) If you find that even just thinking about them brings up strong negative emotions, return to the first question. *But what about me?* Stay with this first question as long as you need to.

You can ask yourself either of these questions any time during the day, especially when thoughts you're having about someone else are taking your attention away from your intention. Always begin with the first question, *But what about me?*

ACKNOWLEDGMENTS

If there was no **Thay**; if there was no **Sister Chan Khong, Sister Tung Nghiem, Sister Huong Nghiem,** and the many other monks and nuns who are also Thay; if I had no home at Parallax (with the support and kindness of **Terry, Travis, Sophie, Terri, Heather,** and **Leslie**); if there wasn't the brilliance and friendship of editor **Tai Moses**; if there was no Publishers Group West (with **Sarah, Elise, Dave,** and many others) dedicated to making sure books got read; if there was no **Debbie Berne** making books beautiful and no **Ericka McConnell** inspiring the best in people; if there was no all-night title commando team also known as family (**Emma, Jon, Tirien, Aminta, Sala,** and **Alan**); if **Sifu Kate** and **Sifu Lynn** did not remind me weekly of the difference between pain and suffering; if the **Salmon River** was not so well loved and taken care of by the **Karuk people** and the **Butler** and **Godfrey** crews; if **Jason, Luna,** and **Plum** were not my True North; and if **Yeshi** and **Osha** had not found each other on the corner of 2nd Avenue and 11th Street in the East Village and run West to make love and milk goats, there would be no me and there would be no book and I would not have this opportunity to say thank you. Thank you dear ones for more than I can possibly say.

PARALLAX PRESS

Parallax Press, a nonprofit organization, publishes books on engaged Buddhism and the practice of mindfulness by Thich Nhat Hanh and other authors. For a copy of the catalog, please contact:

Parallax Press
P.O. Box 7355
Berkeley, CA 94707
Tel: (510) 525-0101
www.parallax.org

RELATED TITLES FROM PARALLAX PRESS

Healing: A Woman's Journey from Doctor to Nun
Sister Dang Nghiem

*Child's Mind: Mindfulness Practices to Help
Our Children Be More Focused, Calm, and Relaxed*
Christopher Willard

Learning True Love: Practicing Buddhism in a Time of War
Sister Chan Khong

Pass it On: Five Stories that Can Change the World
Joanna Macy

Making Space: Creating a Home Meditation Practice
Thich Nhat Hanh

Being Peace
Thich Nhat Hanh

Love in Action: Writings on Nonviolent Social Change
Thich Nhat Hanh